Thoughts are things
Ask, Believe, & Receive

By
Marion Collin

TABLE OF CONTENTS

ACKNOWLEDGMENTS V

LIST OF KEY ELEMENTS VII

PREFACE IX

1. SEEKING THE ANSWER 1
2. SEEKING THE WAY 15
3. SEEKING THE HOW 47
4. SEEKING THE TEACHER 51
5. SEEKING THE LOST GOSPELS 57
6. SEEKING THE POWER - PART I 67
7. SEEKING THE POWER - PART II 77
8. SEEKING THE DOOR 89
9. SEEKING THE WHY 99
10. FINDING AN ANSWER 103
11. TESTING THE ANSWER - PART I 107
12. TESTING THE ANSWER - PART II 113
13. SEEKING OTHER SEEKERS 133
14. SEEKING THE POWER OF THE BRAIN 167
15. GIVING THE ANSWER TO YOU TO TRY 193

16. ASK, BELIEVE, RECEIVE	209
END NOTES:	213
READING LIST	215
APPENDIX I	219
APPENDIX II	223
APPENDIX III	225
APPENDIX IV	229
APPENDIX V	241
ABOUT THE AUTHOR MARION COLLIN	271

Suite 300 - 990 Fort St
Victoria, BC, Canada, V8V 3K2
www.friesenpress.com

Copyright © 2015 by Marion Collin
Glen Collin - Illustrator
Julia Collin - Editor

First Edition — 2015

All rights reserved.

No part of this publication may be reproduced in any form, or by any means, electronic or mechanical, including photocopying, recording, or any information browsing, storage, or retrieval system, without permission in writing from the publisher.

The information contained in this book is intended to be inspirational and educational. It is not intended for treatment, diagnosis or prescription of any health or mental disorder whatsoever. Any information in the book should not replace consultation with a competent healthcare professional. Book content is intended to be used as an adjunct to a rational and responsible healthcare program as prescribed by a healthcare practitioner. The author and publisher specifically disclaim any liability, loss or risk which is incurred as a consequence, directly or indirectly, of the use and application of the contents of this book.

ISBN
978-1-4602-4943-7 (Hardcover)
978-1-4602-4944-4 (Paperback)
978-1-4602-4945-1 (eBook)

1. *Self-Help, Personal Growth*

2. *Self-Help, Spiritual*

Distributed to the trade by The Ingram Book Company

ACKNOWLEDGMENTS

I wish to offer a big thank you to my husband and children who didn't think Mom was too crazy when she said she was writing a book. They all helped in some way. There were also other family and good friends who gave supportive suggestions that greatly enhanced what you are about to read. Thank you all.

LIST OF KEY ELEMENTS

God,

Jesus,

The Aeon Christ,

The Kingdom,

The Power,

Your Brain,

The Soul that is *you*.

PREFACE

Hi Mom

I'm in White Rock with a friend this weekend just hanging out. Funny thing—I just noticed that my hand tremors have stopped. Thought I'd let you know.

Love,

your son.

That simple note above from my son is what started the search for The Answer.

Ask, Believe, and Receive

Is this the Answer to how humankind survives? Do we live the reality created by our own thoughts, by our own "asking"? Or is there more to it?

If there is something more, how do we do this? As our brain is responsible for all our functions, for our thinking, does our brain also help us in some way to ask? Are we wired to communicate? Do we have our own personal intranet?

The Answer has been right in front of humankind all along. What has been lost was the importance of the guidebooks. The map is right there.

1.
SEEKING THE ANSWER

Most of us are seeking an Answer—possibly seeking the Answer to good health; the Answer to happiness; the Answer to wealth; maybe the Answer to spiritual enlightenment.

Where is God? Where is Heaven? Where is the Kingdom? Where is the Path? Does the Path lead to health, to happiness, to wealth? How? What is the driving power?

While reading the Bible's New Testament, it hit me like a ton of bricks—*kerpow!*—right to the middle of the forehead. I *knew* the Answer! There was a Path to follow! There is something important about the words written in red in the Bible: the words of Jesus. It was like a light bulb, a glow, a burst of intense happiness.

In that instant of *kerpow!* I became a seeker. Now I needed to build a platform of support for the thought that was racing through my brain. There were so many pieces to the huge jigsaw puzzle that was now beginning to make much more sense, showing such connectivity.

To start, I was to list as many things as I could remember that I had wished for, prayed for, hoped for, and had somehow received.

There was the happy childhood on the farm with five siblings, all older than me. And I recalled achieving honours throughout grade school while counting the "Reach for the Top" students in high school as my friends, being yearbook editor at tech school, and running for vice president of the student union.

I found the tall man of my dreams in the hallways of that tech school; I married him and had three children. I wanted a boy first, and had that boy, then another boy; then I wished for a girl, and had that baby girl. Having a house in the city, we wanted—and found—a home on a small acreage; we raised the kids in a rural setting, then sent them off to colleges, universities, trade schools. Twenty years later, we moved again.

I always hoped that the acreage beside the highway would bring a good dollar, and it did. The market was high, life was good, and now we wanted to find a good home. We wished for a quiet place, a shop, an upgraded home. We found exactly that, and as we moved, we kept finding more and more that we liked about the valley.

We saw deer, moose, and geese; we also saw beavers, ducks, crocus flowers, and more. It was all there in our valley which had a watershed creek and a beaver dam. As we brought in yet another load of boxes to our new home, I thought, *Seeing a great blue heron in the water would make this perfect*—and we saw one the next day.

Our youngest son gave us a name for our new place: Serenity Valley.

All this happened before knowing the influence that I had over all of these events. Now I realize that some of the sad and worrisome events of my life may also have been brought into my life by none other than me and my thoughts.

In a time of huge despair, I joined a prayer group at church. I'd been a member of the local church choir for many years and was a fairly faithful attendee. I enjoyed singing but had never really quite bought into religion. Choir served a social need; being in a congregation gave me a church family.

But I was in a low mental state at that time, and I cried often; I was on anti-depressants, worked in an unrewarding environment,

THE ANSWER: THOUGHTS ARE THINGS

and despaired over many things. This is what drove me to join the Healing Hearts prayer group. I wasn't sure that I would get anything out of it, but I needed something.

The leader of the group ended the first meeting by asking us to focus on one —and only one—prayer request for the entire week until we met again. We were to pray that prayer daily, and were exhorted to pray deeply.

Our eldest son had hand tremors; he had them for a number of years, but the origin was unknown. Doctors thought he would outgrow them, but he hadn't. I prayed that his hand tremors would stop and go away, and I repeated this prayer each day that week with fervent intensity.

The day before the next Healing Hearts weekly meeting, I received that email from my son saying that he had been away with a friend for the week. "Funny thing," he wrote, "I just noticed that my hand tremors have stopped."

You could have knocked me over with a feather. This was totally unbelievable after all these years. Weeks later, he said they had come back—not as severe, so I was less blown away, but eventually the tremors were controlled; they had not quite stopped and gone away, as asked for in my prayer, but close enough.

This prayer had obviously been directly answered, but how? Why this prayer and not so many others? So I sought the Answer.

I reviewed the setting. The prayer had been done in a private space created in our home. It was a quiet sitting area with a fireplace, surrounded by family photos.

The prayers were done, for the most part, in the quiet of early morning; some were in the quiet of late evening. The prayers were very intentional, with my hands held prayerfully and close

ASK, BELIEVE, & RECEIVE

to my forehead. I focused, starting with the Lord's Prayer; then I stated, "I ask…" I ended the request by saying, "In Jesus' name I pray."

Is this the way? Is this how to communicate with the Lord? The Bible does say to shut yourself away so that you might pray quietly and without interruption. Jesus said:

> *Thou, when thou prayest, enter into thy closet, and when thou hast shut the door, pray to thy Father which is in secret, and thy Father, which seeth in secret, shall reward thee openly.* [Matthew 6:6]. [1].)

Do not pray "shouting" on the street corner. To emphasize this Jesus also said:

> *Thou, when thou prayest, be not as the hypocrites are; for they love to pray standing in the synagogue and in the corners of the streets, that they may be seen of men. Verily I say unto you, they have their reward.* [Matthew 6:5]

This indicates the importance of quiet, meditative thought when praying.

The word *ask* is mentioned in many places throughout the Bible—and not only *ask*, but also *believe* and *receive*. The hand tremors stopped after a daily prayer for one week. My *asking* with strong *believing* resulted in *receiving* for someone other than myself.

Is praying or asking a part of your life? Do you think it could become something you could be comfortable with? Do you feel that you have had an "ask" answered? Write it down here in the space provided.

THE ANSWER: THOUGHTS ARE THINGS

While writing this book, someone close to the family was in a serious accident. The resulting hospitalization and surgeries saved his legs, but one leg was totally rebuilt with plates and pins, the upper part being particularly bad. The other leg was okay down to the top of the knee, but below that were many pins and an ankle replacement. Over the next two years, metal pins and plates broke and had to be replaced. Despite therapy, he did not seem to be able to heal; sharp pain consumed his life.

We talked about his health at a family gathering. He said that in order to cope, he constantly took pain medication. I asked what should I pray for him. He said, "To be whole and healthy." I suggested that he too should ask to be healed.

As we parted later in the day, I gave him a big hug and said, "There—I've taken away all the pain." He said, "Can you handle it? There is a lot of it."

That all occurred on March 30th. The rest of this story follows; this is a copy of the actual texts and emails that we exchanged. (Only the name is changed).

SMS Text: March 31 — 2:05 pm M to L

> Lyel is this still a phone number for you?
>
> Make that Lyle, not Lyel

2:06 pm: L to M

> Yes! Happy Easter Sunday to you!

ASK, BELIEVE, & RECEIVE

2:09 pm M to L

> Ok! Lyle! I was speaking with someone after church today and she said she was really slow healing, too. She is diabetic and said someone with diabetes takes longer to heal. Have you ever been checked for erratic blood sugar levels?

2:11 pm: L to M

> Yes. I am not diabetic. I have a stress hormone.

2:13 pm M to L

> Ok, well, obviously we have to de-stress dat hormone! Is it less stressed in a hot tub or on the beach?

2:15 pm: L to M

> Hmm, that's a tough one. LOL. I'd take a hot tub on a beach! Ha Ha! Sorry, can't answer phone at moment.

2:16 pm: M to L

> Not to worry. I'm headed to basement to do accounting, but I'll keep thinking about you... every day.

2:18 pm: L to M

> Thank you. I appreciate you.

April 2   1:25 pm: L to M

> Believe it or not, I am feeling an amazing amount better! Hard to believe but I haven't felt this good since before the crash.
>
> Pinch me!

SMS Text: 1:41 pm: M to L

Are you serious? I did pray really deep for you and wrote it down in my "Hope" Journal. Well, let's just keep a positive focus. Ask, believe, and receive with gratitude. Thank you, thank you, and thank you. What is your email address? I want to send you something tonight.

1:49 pm: L to M

L...@hotmail.com

1:51 pm: L to M

I am in awe. I'm just... not sure if I dare get hopes up. So live in moment. I am so thankful; no proper words come to mind to say.

2:03 pm: M to L

It is YOU and the power of your brain that is doing this. I'll share tonight. My reality has a happy, whole and healthy Lyle in it. That is what my brain is focusing on through prayer; that is the way in.

2:08 pm: L to M

My mind is open to receive. I have been trying to "will" my body to heal—not asking, then receiving—and I am grateful.

Email April 2

From: M (...@hotmail.com)

Sent April 02, 8:45:01 pm

To: L...@hotmail.com

Hi Lyle,

Finally I'm getting a minute to email you. By the time I ride the LRT, drive a bit, have supper, and do some paperwork, that is just about it for me! Well, young man, you blew me away today with your "I'm feeling an amazing amount better". I've had a lot of prayers answered, but this one was particularly fast!

Lyle, I've been doing a lot of reading about the Power of God, the Power of the Divine that is within each of us. We all carry a cell that was part of the original creator of the earth.

The Secret by Rhonda Byrne is a great book that quotes inspirational leaders giving hope for people, and has some ideas on how to think, meaning to think like you already have something instead of wishing for something. If you wish, that is all you will get; if you think/believe you already have it, you have a better chance of attracting it to you.

But the book didn't quite explain why this works. There is another book called *Science Behind the Secret* by Dr. Travis Taylor that explains how our brains could very likely function like a quantum physics computer. There are nodules in our brains that function like electrical impulses, with up and down and reversing spin cycles.

The human brain could solve a Rubik's cube faster than a computer, because the human brain can see all possibilities at once, whereas at one time a regular computer could only think sequentially and in binary code. Now the computer has caught up, becoming more brain-like.

THE ANSWER: THOUGHTS ARE THINGS

Thoughts are electrical impulses that send out waves that may connect and cohere with other similar waves and hence "attract" to you what you are thinking about. In essence, you attract the reality that you want in your life. This book and *The Secret* are worth a read, or download the DVD from *The Secret* website and buy the Science book.

But, added to that in all my reading, I also came across an article on prayer, and how focused repetitive prayer can create a neural network framework in your brain that makes it easier to have a neural connection to the conscious and unconscious levels of our brain. Focused thought creates this pattern. Basically this is creating a "door in".

I came across another article that was called "the Science of Thank You" that supports the fact that the emotion of gratitude causes the chemical dopamine to be released in the brain. This chemical is associated with happiness and activates the parts of the brain where complex thinking and conflict resolution are thought to reside.

Yet another book — *The Key* by Joe Vitale —describes a method of seeking out the pain and discomfort in your body and "releasing" it. Free your mind and therefore free your body; change your mind and change your body.

Matthew, Luke and Mark in the New Testament quote the words of Jesus—*Ask, believe, receive.*

Here are some other quotes:

"The energy of the mind is the essence of Life."
—Aristotle

"As above, so below; as within, so without."
—*The Emerald Tablet*, circa 3000 B.C.

"Whatsoever ye shall ask in prayer, believing, ye shall receive."
—Matthew 21:22

"What things soever you desire, when ye pray, believe that ye receive them, and ye shall have them."
—Mark 11:24

"Imagination is everything. It is the preview of life's coming attractions."
—Albert Einstein. (Apparently he also said that "Religion without science is blind. Science without religion is lame.")

There is more—much more—and yes, I am writing a book. So you can call me crazy, but here is what I wrote in my gratitude journal (hope journal) on March 31:

"Thank you for today. Thank you for all days. Lord, I ASK that Lyle is completely healed. All pain is gone; he walks well, stands straight, has a healthy sound body and is well-structured.

I ask that he BELIEVES in his good health, that he visualizes his good health. Others have been completely healed. Lyle is completely healed and healthy.

We RECEIVE the good news of Lyle's good health with happiness and thankfulness and gratitude. Thank you for the good health and harmony now flowing through Lyle's body.

Thank you, Father, for you have heard me. I know that you always hear me…"

THE ANSWER: THOUGHTS ARE THINGS

I also prayed, saying the Lord's Prayer very slowly and ending by adding basically the same thing as I had written: *ask*, *believe* and *receive*.

I also visualized, as I went to sleep that night, looking deep into your eyes and going inside you, looking for the pain and telling it to go away, to be all healthy tissue.

So did it work, maybe? I'd say quite possibly yes. Or was it something that became a light bulb in your own brain?

Whatever—let's enjoy, let's celebrate!

But I tell you, I am becoming more and more convinced that thoughts are things; watch what you think!

Now I'm working on attracting immense wealth. Repeat after me: I am healthy, happy, and wealthy. Better yet, I am healthy, happy, wealthy and in a hot tub on the beach!

Love you much. Very glad you are feeling better.

Email April 3

> *To: M (.....@hotmail.com)*
>
> *From Lyle (...@hotmail.com)*
>
> *Sent: April 03, 5:21:30 a.m.*

You—I am thankful for you, your spirit, your heart, your kindness, compassion, and true being. I believe I have angels with me at all times, I know this to be true. I feel, I hear, I have seen.

You are my first real walking, breathing angel. Why have I not noticed you? I see so much more than I dare speak of, as I am not crazy, but some may think so. I am open to all things; I focus on the power of good. You are an absolute blessing in my life.

All you have said has electrocuted my insides! I know, I understand all you said. I don't know why 'I' see all I do; it's taken me many years to see it's a gift. I do not know how to use it.

You warm my heart and fill my eyes with how much I matter to you; I am unbelievably touched by you, what you say for me. Your soul is golden.

All that is good and pure and righteous shall come to you; I believe you are all of this. I have not seen colours for so long. I have been bitter, closed off. I am so happy now!

Like I said, I feel you gave my inner soul an electric shock/boost (I don't know how to explain—sorry). I feel zero pain. ZERO! I feel like I have run a marathon, and I am stiff and so sore, but it is a normal ache.

I told my friend that I remember how it feels to have legs that hurt and ache. But there is no knife-cutting pain inside. It's strange: my ankle feels wrapped tight, like it won't move, but the pain is gone; it's just stiff.

In the last two days, I have woken up and stood in shock, not sure if I should take a step and be back to before, in pain. It's overwhelming and I'm at a loss for words.

I am going to go ride a pedal bike outside tomorrow. Seriously. I am!

THE ANSWER: THOUGHTS ARE THINGS

You are amazing, and are truly an inspiration. I am thankful for you!

I don't want to sleep; I am cleaning, rejoicing in the freedom of being pain free. I'm floating. I can go on and on. Honestly, I don't know if I should laugh or cry. I'm just happy, thankful and so much more.

Love you so very, very much. I'm living in the WOW factor. LOL!

Lyle

Well, all that certainly sat me down. Did I actually help bring healing to this man through prayer and so quickly? I'm still in shock. I think I just inspired him and he healed himself. He is still working on complete health as now all those plates and pins that are in his legs will be removed, but I have faith that there will be good results.

Do you have a friend or family member that you are worried about? Write down their name and why you are concerned about them.

_____
_____
_____
_____
_____
_____

2.
SEEKING THE WAY

I started my search by reading book after book on the powers of prayer and meditation. To give some idea of what books I was drawn to read, here is an excerpt from an email to a colleague who was intrigued by my search.

> Hi Bob,
>
> Reading the book *The Secret* by Rhonda Byrne was very inspirational so I thought a good starting point for reading would be the various authors and participants that contributed to the book and the DVD that was produced.
>
> I started with some of the authors from the late 1800s and early 1900s but also found some very recent "still-alive" authors who were writing on why the law of attraction works. Some books try to explain how far back in time this "law" goes.
>
> Other books "discover" quantum physics and the possibility that our very own brains contain components similar to quantum physics, like computers. Mankind had never been able to make a computer capable of doing quantum physics, though they may be closer to achieving that now. Doctors and scientists have never been able to transplant the brain from one body to another, except in sci-fi movies. Our brains are our own.
>
> Many "still-alive" authors have written books giving really good tools for actually using the law

of attraction, removing doubt, "allowing" things to happen and using the vibration (energy) circle that surrounds you. These books help you identify good vibes and bad vibes and how to manage your feeling around them. Some give you good clues, such as to how to make really descriptive vision boards to stimulate the right side of the brain (the right brain may be a more direct link to your subconscious).

If you can get into these types of books, you will have a huge grip on the concept of watching what you think, as you create your own future.

The books encourage you to dwell only on what you want to happen. Push away the bad and negative thoughts; replace them with happy thoughts.

Don't say "I wish"— say "I have." Otherwise, you will only ever wish.

Many sayings refer to the power of the mind, the imagination, and of life being changed by thoughts:

"All that we are is the result of what we have
thought. The mind is everything. What we think, we become."
—Buddha

"Be careful how you think. Your life is shaped by your thoughts."
—Proverbs 4:23

These quotes are everywhere if you look for them.

Other books give you tools to keep the energy and attraction level up by being thankful for what you have, and thankful "in the present tense" for what you want to have.

THE ANSWER: THOUGHTS ARE THINGS

There are books on understanding the conscious, subconscious, and super-subconscious (Universal Mind) and still more that advocate mental healing, metaphysical thought, and abundance for all. Some provide step-by-step tools to help your brain direct thoughts, and direct energy. Many advocate that the science of thinking and attracting is the key to life. Most of these books suggest some good tools to make you think.

An entirely different pathway of books has been to read authors seeking connectivity between science and Christian thought. There are ministers of faith seeking scientific answers, and there are scientists becoming ministers, because science does not answer it all for them. They speak about the presence of a new regime in the world—perhaps a regime that could perform miracles through the power of the mind.

Many books speak of metaphysics and quantum physics. They advocate that science and religion must go together to attain the deepest understanding. This exact thinking dates back to the philosophers and scientists from 600 BC.

The book that I've spent a lot of time on is the Bible – King James Version, the words of Jesus Christ are written in red. Jesus was the messenger. Reading His words alone takes away the background descriptions written by others. If these truly are the words of Jesus as the messenger trying to tell us something, they are very important words that are worth revisiting. A key might be "Seek ye first the Kingdom of God".

Of note here, too, is the fact that Jesus was reputed to have gone off by himself a lot to pray for guidance before performing miracles; it is written that he could only perform miracles on those that believed He could do those miracles.

There are many more books yet to read—books on health, wealth and happiness and achieving them all.

I'm not quite ready to share *The Answer*; it still a bit like a pot of soup—always simmering. I will say that in all these books that I have been reading, I've not quite seen in their writing, the same path that I see; if someone is on the same wavelength, they haven't written a book, or I haven't found the book on it yet!

I have learned from these books the importance of mindfulness meditation. This practice promotes a calm and stable mindset. The best and clearest thinking occurs while in a relaxed mind set. Now I need the time to just sit and practice this clear thinking.

Would appreciate hearing from you, if you have any "revelations". And I will say it again: One of the strongest things you can do is to start writing things down; date them.

Look back and think about events that happened after you had hoped they would.

Think and write down things that you would like to happen. Use words similar to the following:

With this prayer I ASK that I have_____. Other people have this. I BELIEVE that I have it too. I RECEIVE this _____with happiness and a smile.

I think you should also add "In Jesus' name I pray", but you may or may not be comfortable with that.

Remember, your brain doesn't always separate what you are imagining from what is really occurring. An example is testing athletes "imagining" their event; the same thought patterns and muscles fire as if they were actually "doing" the event. So pretending is good.

I have found it amazing the number of times I've read over things I've written and found they have come to be—some things that have been prayed for, and some things that have just been deeply thought about.

Enjoy! I'm not crazy... just certifiable."

So that was my letter to Bob quite early on in my search. As you can see, there are a lot of intriguing books—great books with huge knowledge, written by great thinkers. I still have a list of "yet-to-read" books. I've also been led to read other books and articles; they just seem to show up in my path.

More and more it was becoming clear to me that the power of prayer could actually be linked with the power of the brain.

I seem to be most drawn to the "Big Book"—the Holy Bible. The Bible speaks of prayer and seeking knowledge, over and over again in both the Old and New Testament.

> "Hear the word of the Lord..."
> —Hosea 4:1

> "My people are destroyed for lack of knowledge."
> —Hosea 4:6

> "Reprove one that hath understanding, and he will understand knowledge."
> —Proverbs 19:25

> "And I saw a new heaven and a new earth, for the first heaven and the first earth were passed away."
> —Revelations 21:1

What are these parables? What do they mean?

As I mentioned previously, I am most intrigued by the words in red print as I wanted to "hear" the exact words that Jesus spoke. What messages was he trying to impart to us, to humankind?

Why did he focus on teaching mankind to seek knowledge, to think and to pray? I wanted to print them in red in this book, but learned that it would vastly increase the cost of printing, so any time that the Biblical spoken words of Jesus are quoted; they are in bold, italicized and underlined. This is to clearly identify them from other quotes that are in this book. Please read them with the intent to seek his inner meaning.

As a minister had pointed out, the Jesus words are the ones that most scholars and historians agree have the highest probability of being his actual words.

Jesus said:

> ***"Search the scriptures, for in them ye think ye have eternal life, and they are they which testify of me."*** —John 5:39

> ***"How shall ye believe my words?"***
> —John 5:47

THE ANSWER: THOUGHTS ARE THINGS

"If ye abide in me, and my words abide in you, ye shall ask what ye will, and it will be done unto you." —John 15:7

"Greater things than these shall ye do." —John 1:50

"I am come that they might have life, and that they might have it more abundantly." —John 10:10

What was Jesus trying to tell us?

- "Testify"
- "Believe"
- "Ask"
- "It will be done"
- "Abundant life."

The words seem to be giving instructions to follow.

How to search? The starting point might be the words in the Lord's Prayer. That prayer was quite specifically given to mankind to be "prayed" so it must be an important portal. The Scriptures are full of parables. Was there hidden meaning to be found in these words?

> *Our Father, who art in Heaven, Hallowed be thy name; thy Kingdom come...*

I spent quite some time creating my own library of scripture quotes that refer to *Heaven, Kingdom,* and *Hallowed,* and also scripture quotes that might contain the words *ask, believe,* and *receive.*

A lot of work went into it; I even downloaded the entire Bible (the Authorized or King James Version) to an Excel spreadsheet to use the "Find" function to search for these words. Then I was talking about this project with a friend and Jan said, "Why don't you use the Concordance at the back of the Bible?" Ha! I didn't even know that was back there! So yes—I switched to the concordance for a number of the words being researched.

However, the Excel Bible is still useful for finding things. It is really quite a handy tool—an "electronic Bible". You might try it for yourself.

"Our Father, who art in Heaven…"

Where is God? Where is Heaven? Could it be that with the creation of the universe with all its stars and planets, the Creative Spirit was embedded into all living things? The Spirit is embedded even more deeply into sentient "thinking" beings. Does each of us carry one individual cell that is God-like? Instead of praying to God above, should we pray to God within?

What is "Heaven"? Is Heaven abundant with health, wisdom, and wealth?

> "He that hath a <u>bountiful</u> eye shall be blessed"
> —Proverbs 22:9

> "And Abram was very <u>rich</u> in cattle, in <u>silver</u>, and in <u>gold</u>."
> —Genesis 13:2

> "Then shalt thou lay-up <u>gold</u> as dust, and the <u>gold</u> of Ophir as the stones of the brooks."
> —Job 22:24

THE ANSWER: THOUGHTS ARE THINGS

> "Yea, the Almighty shall be thy defence, and thou shalt have plenty of <u>silver</u>."
> —Job 22:25

> "And Ephraim said, yet I am become <u>rich</u>, I have found me out <u>substance</u>."
> —Hosea 12:8

What do you see as the connecting words of these parables? Do they speak of poverty?

_____

_____

_____

> "So king Solomon exceeded all the kings of the earth for <u>riches</u> and for <u>wisdom</u>"
> —Third Book of Kings 10:23

> "For <u>wisdom</u> *is* a defence *and* <u>money</u> *is* a defence: but the Excellency of <u>knowledge</u> *is, that* <u>wisdom giveth life to them that have it</u>."
> —Ecclesiastes 7:12

It appears that the advice was to stock up on the local currency (that being cattle, silver, and gold). Wisdom and knowledge "giveth life". Not all were poor shepherds; many living in the era of the Old Testament were well off. But how did they do it? Were they following some special instructions? Did they know some secret? Is the secret that wisdom giveth Life? What is wisdom? Could wisdom mean thinking? Is that the Answer? That thinking giveth Life?

> "Hast thou heard the <u>secret of God</u>? and dost thou restrain <u>wisdom</u> to thyself?"
> —Job 15:8

23

"But where shall <u>wisdom</u> be found? And where *is* the place of understanding?"
—Job 28:12

"Whence then cometh <u>wisdom</u>? and where *is* the place of understanding?"
—Job 28:20

"Happy *is* the man *that* findeth <u>wisdom</u>, and the man *that* getteth understanding."
—Proverbs 3:13

"<u>Wisdom</u> *is* the principal thing; *<u>therefore</u> <u>get wisdom</u>*: and with all thy getting get understanding." —Proverbs 4:7

"If any of you <u>lack wisdom, let him ask of God</u>, that giveth to all men liberally, and upbraideth not; <u>and it shall be given him.</u>"
—James 1:5

What word do you see repeated again and again? Now substitute thinking for the word wisdom in readings above. What do you think these scriptures are telling you?

_____
_____
_____

"But let him ask in faith, nothing wavering."
—James 1:6

"…How much more shall your heavenly Father give the Holy Spirit to them that ask him?"
—Luke 11:13

THE ANSWER: THOUGHTS ARE THINGS

Jesus answered and said unto them, **"Verily I say unto you, If ye have faith, and doubt not, ye shall not only do this which is done to the fig tree, but also if ye shall say unto this mountain, Be thou removed, and be thou cast into the sea; it shall be done."**
—Matthew 21:21

"Then they took away the stone *from the place* where the dead was laid. And Jesus lifted up *his* eyes, and said, **"Father, I thank thee that thou hast heard me."**
—John 11:41

Wow, what was all that? Well, they were quotes from the Bible—a lot from the Old Testament, and some from the New Testament being the actual words spoken by Jesus.

They all seem to imply that we might have some control over our choices for our life if we have "knowledge", have thinking. Not only that, but also that life is to be abundant with wisdom and riches. Search. Seek wisdom; say thank you.

Is this the pathway? Is the journey, the seeking, as important as the wisdom found? Is that the secret? Is that the Answer? While we are searching and seeking should we also be asking and thinking?

Very interesting train of thought, isn't it? Let's just step back, way back out of the sand box.

Once upon a time...

How did we start this dialogue? Oh yes, the Beginning!

"In the beginning was the Word..."
—John 1.1

In the beginning, God had the "Word"; He had "imagination".

Was this Word, this imagination, this thinking, the preview that created the first spark to create the first life?

> "And the Word was made flesh…"
> —John 1:14.

Perhaps the Words were,

> "'Let there be light', and there was light"
> —Genesis 1:3

Hold onto that thought about "light" and what it might mean.

Dr. Travis Taylor's book, *Science Behind the Secret,* has a really good section on light and how it can be called light waves or light particles. Light behaves as a wave until it is seen, and then it becomes a particle. This concept is very thought-provoking. Could light be a foundational substance? But Taylor says mainly that light is light and that you have to accept it as that.

If you could direct light waves to create specifically shaped particles, what shapes would you create?

_____
_____
_____

The Man Project Part I

Let's pretend that we are an all-powerful being—spirit, energy, a great omnipotent deity—and we want to create something big, something permanent, something evolving, self-sustaining and independently functioning.

THE ANSWER: THOUGHTS ARE THINGS

So, in the beginning was the thought and the Word. How about the words *Big Bang?* Almost all scientists agree there was "something" that started the universe as we are coming to know it. A popular cartoon book series derided the lack of imagination used by the scientists in naming one of the most phenomenal events ever as the Big Bang. The book went on to suggest that it should be called something like The Great Big Super Kala Fristic Space Kazam. But instead we have "Big Bang". Oh, well.

So the all-powerful Spirit, the Great Omnipotent Deity, thought up a plan, "imagined it as it should be" and spoke the "Word". I am thinking the word might be "ENERGY!" Ka-Boom! A massive energy explosion caused the cosmic activity, creating suns, planets, moons, the Milky Way, all swishing, filling the empty black void.

Wow! That was quite the word! How could a thought, a word, be so powerful?

But now what? There were pretty colours, but there was not much happening; there was still emptiness.

There was more to the Plan. The Great Omnipotent Deity had big things in mind. Was the third rock from the star (the sun) picked deliberately or accidentally? Did it have the right potential, the right distance from its heat-radiating sun? Regardless, as the rock cooled down, water and oxygen was created.

> "When God began creating the heavens and the
> earth, the earth was at first a shapeless, chaotic
> mass, with the Spirit of God brooding over the dark
> vapours."
> —Genesis 1:1-2

> "Then God said, 'Let there be light' and light
> appeared. And God was pleased with it, and divided

> the light from the darkness. So he let it shine for a while, and then there was darkness again. He called the light 'daytime' and the darkness 'nighttime'. Together they formed the first day."
> —Genesis 1:3

These excerpts are from "The Living Bible" paraphrased. [2].) It is interesting that there was a footnote explaining "day" as being "one day" or "one period of time". This hints at a thought to ponder: "How long is God's day?" Could it be one revolution of earth around the sun? Perhaps a "God-day" could be several million years or more, with each day being one revolution around of the entire universe.

Change your perception of a "day" to being several million or billion years; it opens up many more possibilities. If the universe burst into existence fourteen billion years ago and a "God-day" is two billion years long, we are only in day seven now—the day of rest.

Sky and oceans were separated in a "period of time" on God-day two; dry land with plants and trees emerged on the third "period of time" or God-day.

> "The LORD by wisdom hath founded the earth; by understanding hath he established the heavens"
> —Proverbs 3:19

Land masses arose. After all the rumbling, it was pretty quiet—less empty, but lifeless.

A lot of discussion by scientists has occurred around how life started; the theory is that it most likely began in the sea. But how did the first cell get started, and how did the first two cells of creation get introduced and start creating life?

THE ANSWER: THOUGHTS ARE THINGS

Could it be that the Great Omnipotent Deity had the "thought" of living beings in mind, and once more, in the beginning was the "thought" and the "Word"? This Word and action caused the first two cells of the simplest life form, the amoeba, to combine, split and grow.

The odds of this happening accidentally are astronomically impossible without Divine intervention.

These simple-celled creatures grew and became more complex. They had no thinking capability but functioned at a subconscious level. Subconsciously they strived, thrived, and made adaptations. To find food and to evade predators, these creatures evolved and developed; they transitioned in the sea and eventually crawled out of the ocean; they developed wings, flew, and climbed trees.

The evolution of creatures, reptiles, and then mammals was a long, slow process over millions of years, and over a whole "period of time". Evolutionists believe that mammals evolved from chimpanzees to become modern-day mankind.

Although these theories have a lot of validity, archaeological findings do not yet fully support the final link between the DNA make-up of the ape with the upright walking sentient being now called "man"—a being with a very complex brain, and with a very complex full color spectrum eyesight. Humans have eyesight that gives them 180 degrees of forward facing horizontal vision. With eyeball rotation and peripheral vision this increases to 270 degrees. All that is seen by the human eye in any instant is immediately processed by the brain. If we have developed into such complex organisms as the result of an evolutionary accident, will the end of mankind also be an evolutionary accident? Or is there an all-encompassing plan?

Could it be possible that the Great Omnipotent Deity got to thinking that things were not moving along quite fast enough with the evolution method? Perhaps the Great Omnipotent Deity could see that the jump from ape to man was genetically not going to happen soon without intervention.

So let us give Creationists a paragraph, too. Again, a quote from The Living Bible Paraphrased:

> "Then God said, 'Let the waters teem with fish and other life and let the skies be filled with birds of every kind.'"
> —Genesis 1:20
>
> "And God said, 'Let the earth bring forth every kind of animal.'"
> —Genesis 1:24
>
> "Then God said, 'Let us make a man—someone like ourselves' to be the master of all life upon the earth and in the skies and in the seas.'"
> —Genesis 1:26

This takes us up to the end of the sixth day or "period of time".

Perhaps the Great Omnipotent Deity did have The Thought and spoke The Word that did indeed create man in "His" or "Our" image. Maybe we were literally crafted directly from clay; or perhaps it was figuratively from clay, using the material already started from clay by evolution, then adding a little tweaking of the cranial cavity, enhancement of the eye function, and implantation of a smoothly-running subconscious to run all the body parts.

Then came the added touch of a thinking, conscious mind in a powerful brain. These added components were the last crowning touches, making the jump to a thinking sentient being—mankind. This man "in His image" had a brain with the processing capability similar to the technology of a most ingenious computer. In

THE ANSWER: THOUGHTS ARE THINGS

fact, this man was equipped with such a fascinating processing unit that it has not been truly duplicated to this day.

The Living Bible says,

> "Then God looked over all that he had made, and it was excellent in every way. This ended the sixth day [period of time]."
> —Genesis 1:31

In the beginning was the Word, and the Word became flesh, and man was created in "His" own image, implying in God's own image. This gives a sense of being built for not only one lifetime, but being built to last for eternity as part of an eternal plan. An overall plan makes sense—otherwise one might pose the same question as did the astrophysicist Stephen Hawking: "Why does the universe go to all the bother of existing?"

Wow! Double wow!

So, this "in the beginning" episode is to try to get you thinking that there was a "beginning". Energy is neither created nor destroyed; it only changes form. This is the law of conservation of energy and the first law of thermodynamics. Because energy only changes form, in each of us a cell, an atom or an electron has descended to *you* from the very first cell that was there right at the very beginning. This is a profound and powerful thought!

Each of us is part of the beginning of life, and we are made in the image of the most powerful "Starter of Life".

What if you indeed did have an original creation cell? Would it make you feel different about yourself and others? Circle one below:

                  Yes   No   Maybe

The Man Project Part II

We are still talking about early man, but now we will explore the idea of a "thinking" man.

Was the intent of the Great Omnipotent Deity just to have a basic thinking man, or did the episode in the Garden of Eden change things? The instructions were basic: "You may eat of any fruit in the garden except fruit from the Tree of Conscience." (Living Bible, paraphrased, Genesis 2:16) The Holy Bible Authorized King James version specifies that any fruit in the garden could be eaten, "…. but of the tree of knowledge." (Genesis 1:17).

The fruit was eaten and, whether by intention or otherwise, the Great Omnipotent Deity now had a being that had conscious and unconscious thoughts and knowledge.

The Bible story of the Garden of Eden may have roots in the myth of a poem of great antiquity called the Gilgamesh Epic. Elements of this fall of man myth describe Enkidu being shunned by wild creatures and of a priestess covering his nakedness. There is also an Akkadian myth of Adapa that has the theme of the serpent's warning to Eve.

So here are ancient stories that sound a lot like the Garden of Eden story, and yet were passed on from much earlier than the Bible was written. They must have been very important and foundational stories to have been passed on through generations of mankind.

The mythmaking process is a method of describing new situations by using a reflective, conscious application of older myths. The Babylonian and Canaanite cultures had the presence of myths in their cultures. The Bible also has the presence of myths. Ancient Israel and its mythmaking formed the biblical tradition.

Just as the New Testament is an accumulation of stories of apostles, disciples, and prophets from the time of Jesus and after, the Old Testament is an accumulation of stories from ancient peoples from the ages prior to the time of Jesus. We have to thank the Hebrew scholars and savants for the efforts made to capture these stories and myths and to translate them into text for us to study. The King James Version of the Bible itself is five linguistic removes from the first bibles written. This English version being a translation of the Greek Version which was a translation from the Aramaic and Hebrew. What was written in the original originals is quite unknown now. The 1609 translation commissioned by King James was edited by Sir Francis Bacon (1561-1626) a genius of his time with many talents including possibly writing prose & poetry under the pen name of Shake-Speare. Francis Bacon had been initiated into the Order of the Knights Templar and privy to the knowledge of secret words and secret knowledge. It is thought that in his editing of the King James translation he may have imbedded through secret code this knowledge into the scripts of the Old and New Testament. This makes the search for a pathway, an Answer even more intriguing.

Yes, some stories may have been "interpreted" by the writers, therefore not correctly reflecting the message and some meanings may have been lost in translation, but at least the words are here for us to study, to question, and to accept or reject according to our individual discernment.

There is the possibility that the original intent for "The Man Project" had dramatically changed. The intent may have been to create a gardener whose only role was to tend the Garden of God—end of story; now that plan was thwarted.

If Scripture is to be believed, man and woman now had the same knowledge as God. Did the Tree of Conscience give man and woman a "soul"? Is the soul the key to our inner being, the essence of who and what we are?

> "Behold, the man is become as one of us."
> —Genesis 3:22

Who is this "us"? It is a clear statement that has survived the translations of ancient myths and the passage of time.

Again, let's step back and perhaps put *you* into the plan, cast in the role of the Great Omnipotent Deity. You could not guide every activity, every individual thing in the new world you had just created. Or maybe you could. Being omnipotent and omniscient you could indeed do all this thinking for each individual but as the Great Omnipotent Deity you chose to have this man creature be independent with his own thoughts. You therefore created thinking beings capable of having free will, free volition, to come up with their own ideas for their own lives.

The solution was to provide for them the material, the thinking substance, the energy in which the Being's thoughts could be placed to attract to them the environment they wanted, the abundance of life. Could light be part of that thinking substance?

This was the knowledge and power that the Great Omnipotent Deity had. After all, you had thought the Thought, spoken the Word, and created the world using that very same thinking substance; you couldn't have *every* thinking human on earth doing that—could you? Or maybe you could...

Through your created being's own thought, could they sustain themselves? Create their own world and you could live and feel what they were experiencing, living vicariously through the created beings. The ultimate gift is to see a child live well, live with prosperity, live happily. Health, wealth and happiness!

THE ANSWER: THOUGHTS ARE THINGS

What a dream, what a thought—a self-sustaining world, with self-sustaining beings, and with the same power as their Creator to create their own reality. Is this the power of God? To live? To be? Is this the Answer?

Wow! Triple wow!

What do you think about that? Is this thinking really a possibility?

Circle one:

                Yes   No   Maybe

With that question in mind, consider this: the man you had created had now eaten of the Tree of Knowledge prior to receiving instructions on how to use this knowledge, this Power.

Why wouldn't the Great Omnipotent Deity want man to have full knowledge? Did He think that man was not ready yet?

The beings would have the same power as you, the Great Omnipotent Deity, their Creator, the One that had "thought" them up in order to thrive. But would that be too much too soon?

This was the catch, and perhaps you (as the Great Omnipotent Deity) could not yet trust man to handle the Power properly. As a precaution, you hid the Power so that man would have to seek it, and through seeking, would eventually find it. This would have man better placed to control the Power within.

There was a little story in some of my readings about where this great secret was hidden—not on the highest mountain, not in the deepest valley, not in the farthest reaches of the earth nor the deepest ocean. To keep man from finding the greatest secret, it was hidden where he would never find it "deep inside himself".

So just where could "deep inside" be?

Let's step back into the story. Let's imagine that the Great Omnipotent Deity did just that—hid the secret of the power deep in the brain of man, and left man and his mate to start a new world of sentient beings.

He wanted his man-child to learn the power, but how could He instruct them? Leaving rules didn't really work the first round. When they were in the Garden of Eden, He had said, "Don't eat from the Tree of Conscience (Knowledge)." Well, we all know how that worked out with the fruit and all.

The Great Omnipotent Deity often spoke directly to man, and as time went on, He did so in speaking to a great leader in order to instruct the people. This man, known as Moses, brought down commandments to provide guidance. These were on two stone tablets "written with the finger of God" (Exodus 31:18). The commandments were basic rules to encourage order and structure. The first four are religious in nature with the remaining six being moral laws to help govern man's behavior to others. A basic do onto others as you would do unto yourself theme.

Another great leader that He spoke to was named Abram: "I will make of thee a great nation, Abram, and in thee all nations be blessed." This was one of several promises which came to be known as the Covenant.

Over the years, there were a number of great leaders and prophets trying to follow the Word of the Great Omnipotent Deity. They were trying to have righteousness or "right thinking". However, most of mankind still was proceeding through life without guidance, without seeking to follow the Covenant or the Commandments. What to do?

In those thousands of years, spiritual guidance had constantly been given to all that would listen and seek. Mankind had definitely evolved, but the Great Omnipotent Deity was dismayed at the direction in which mankind was headed. Many indulged in states of intoxication, debauchery, and in worshipping all sorts of graven idols.

The solution was to have one good man and his family build a boat, and to round up two of every animal, bird, and all creatures that had evolved. Then the Great Omnipotent Deity caused the waters to flood the entire land mass, ending all sentient life—except for the family of Noah. This was a fresh start on "The Man Project".

Everyone on earth is a descendant of the evolved/created Adam and Eve, but maybe only through Noah, depending on whether one land mass or all land masses are believed to be flooded. The Bible clearly implies all-encompassing flood, some ancient myths allude to massive rivers flooding. "Go now and multiply; go now and start again," said the Great Omnipotent Deity. He did not just take off to pay attention to some other project. This was another chance for humanity, but it was specifically a project that needed constant guidance in the developing of its power, united in the belief in one God, and no other.

Yes, the Old Testament may be based on myths of ancient peoples, but the stories must have been important as they were passed on and on through many generations to eventually be documented in text to be read by all. The ancient myths mention a flood but details are vague as to how big of a flood. The myths also mention warning Noah. For the sceptics reading this, remnants of the ark may well have been found in mountains in Europe, and the origin of most plant life in the world can be traced back to originating from that same area.

Do you think that these ancient myths could be true and that there truly was an ark? Have you thought about why the myths were passed on from generation to generation? Write your thoughts below.

_____

_____

_____

The Man Project Part III

The Great Omnipotent Deity realized he had to bring a prophet into the world—a teacher who would come to this planet called Earth. He would be a teacher that would be believed and followed—a teacher who would impress and teach His earth descendants, His created children to seek the knowledge and the power that was inherently built into them but that so few had discovered. This teacher was to help them find their thinking power.

Whether you believe that Jesus is the "son" of God or that he is only a great prophet, Jesus did exist and he discovered or was gifted with the power to perform miracles.

But before we get to that, let's talk about divinity, ancient faiths, and ancient scholars who believed in the divinity of man. Here is a description about where the power of God was hidden:

According to an old Hindu legend, there was a time when all men were gods, but they so abused their divinity that Brahma, the chief god, decided to take it away from men and hide it where they would never again find it. Where to hide it became the big question.

When the lesser gods were called in council to consider the question, they said, 'We will bury man's divinity deep in the earth.' But

THE ANSWER: THOUGHTS ARE THINGS

Brahma said, 'No that will not do; for man will dig deep down into the earth and find it.'

Then they said, 'Well, we will sink his divinity into the deepest ocean.' But again Brahma replied, 'No, not there, for man will learn to dive into the deepest waters, will search out the ocean bed, and will find it.'

Then the lesser gods said, 'We will take it to the top of the highest mountain and there hide it.' But again Brahma replied, 'No, for man will eventually climb every high mountain on earth. He will be sure some day to find it and take it up again for himself.'

Then the lesser gods gave up and concluded, 'We do not know where to hide it, for it seems there is no place on earth or in the sea that man will not eventually reach.'

Then Brahma said, 'Here is what we will do with man's divinity. We will hide it deep down in man himself, for he will never think to look for it there.' Ever since then, the legend concludes, man has been going up and down the earth, climbing, digging, diving, exploring, searching for something that is already in himself. [3].)

The search for divinity has been a constant in the evolution of man. Between the ancient history of the Old Testament and the less ancient history of the New Testament is a whole section of other seekers of knowledge, of divinity.

3000 BC and prior

Ancient Jainism or Jain theology originated in the Indus Valley civilization of India. The basis was the lifestyle of the Tirthankaras who achieved enlightenment of perfect knowledge through practicing restraint in the actions of speech, body and mind. The leader, Rishabha, led the movement of Jainism's teaching that living beings had a divine soul, were capable of *infinite perception*, *infinite knowledge, infinite power, and were capable of finding infinite happiness.* Rishabha taught that through right conduct, right view, and right knowledge, each soul was the architect of its own life in this reality and any other reality.

These teachings later evolved into belief in dharma, being a belief in universal truth and the ultimate reality of the universe. Actions shape your past, present, and future experiences, being the karma, a metaphysical force of nature shaping the dharma. The Hindu faith developed the idea of reincarnation, that some soul or spirit or higher true self remains after death to be made flesh again along the lines that energy can neither be created nor destroyed.

In Egypt (3000–2300 BC), ancient religious texts were carved on pyramid walls saying things such as there are no limits to where the spirit can go. What had the Egyptians experienced that they would write this on their pyramid walls? The Egyptian Goddess Ma'at was the goddess of universal truth, ethics, cosmic balance and order.

Here are faiths that are thousands of years old advocating that it is our own soul that creates the reality that we live in and that soul of ours has no limits.

2500–1000 BC
The time of Abraham (2500–1000 BC) brought forth the belief in monotheism—one God, as well as a belief in prophets and that there was a divine law guiding the morals and ethics of followers. This formed the basis for the Abrahamic religions of Samaritans, Judaism, Islam, Druze ad, Christianity and later religions such as the Rastafarians. Worshipping one God should mean that all of these faiths follow the one great law, "Thou shalt not avenge nor bear any grudge against the children of thy people, but thou

THE ANSWER: THOUGHTS ARE THINGS

shalt love thy neighbour as thyself: I am the LORD." (Leviticus 19:18) This was written from the instructions God gave to Moses, or may even be from much earlier, during the time of the Judean monarchy in 7th century BC. A law with such deep roots should be taken to heart.

1000–0 BC

Confucius (K'ung Fu-tzu) (551–479 BC) taught that studying and learning about the universe was the path to enlightenment, to understanding. He also advocated the greatest law of love your neighbour through the statement, "Do unto others as you would have done unto yourself."

Buddhism came out of the enlightenment of Siddhartha Gautama (563–483 BC) that the origin of suffering is ignorance and due to an unclear mind. He advocated right thought, right speech, right action, right understanding with right concentration and right mindfulness. These right processes would clear the mind and assist connectivity with the past, present and future. You can see that the basis of this appears to come from the ancient Jain theology. A lot of modern day mindfulness meditations support the clearing of the mind and clearing your thinking for a healthy well balanced life.

Philosophers:
Thales (624–546 BC)

At the same time as the religious movements were evolving, great philosophers were also pondering divinity. The Greek philosopher Thales of Miletus believed that divinity perpetuated not only through deities but through mankind, thus creating the philosophy of the universal mind. He also developed and promoted the idea that "space is the greatest thing, as it contains all things". He was referring to empty space. Is empty space the thinking substance? This is yet another profound and powerful thought!

Pythagoras (570–495 BC)
Pythagoras of Samos was a Greek philosopher but also a scientist and mathematician (and the creator of the Pythagorean Theorem). He felt the language of math could describe the universe and suggested that science and religion were "inseparable." He postulated that the brain, not the heart, was the source of thought, and he was one of the first to teach that the earth was spherical and revolved around the sun. His travels took him on a journey to Egypt; he spent time amongst the Chaldeans and Magian teaching himself geometry, astronomy, principles of religion, ethics and conduct. He founded the religious movement called Pythagoreanism and the Pythagorean Brotherhood, each having secretive rites and symbolism. The society studied mathematics and logical reasoning as opposed to religious dogma. Rosicrucianism and Freemasonry both have their roots in this society.

We now know that the source of thoughts is in the brain, but 2,600+ years ago this was not common knowledge. Pythagoras may have been considered a radical for even suggesting this.

Socrates (469–399 BC)
There should be no doubt that, despite his claim to know only that he knew nothing, Socrates had great knowledge and strong beliefs about the divine. Endless studying is the path to wisdom. The Socrates method is to take a difficult problem and break it down into smaller questions until the original problem could be solved. Socrates was interested in the idea that something could be real even if it did not have a physical Form.

THE ANSWER: THOUGHTS ARE THINGS

Socrates held that the world of Forms is transcendent to our own world (the world of substances). Forms are both spatial and temporal meaning they are transcendent to space, have no spatial dimensions, have no orientation in space, are the essential basis of reality and do not exist within any time period. Forms are to be considered the most pure and perfect of all things being neither eternal, existing forever, nor mortal, of limited duration. Furthermore, he believed that true knowledge/intelligence is the ability to grasp the world of Forms with one's mind. How can we do this? How to grasp nonphysical forms with our mind?

Both Socrates and his student Plato believed that there were levels of divine inspiration, higher concepts and higher realities.

Plato (428-387 BC)

Plato postulated in his Theory of Forms that the material world is a shadow of the real world. Many modern day authors also speak of the material world being a shadow of the real world. Here is Plato advocating it 400 years before the time of the Æon Christ.

Ideas and thoughts are to be considered the fundamental form of reality not the material world of change that we know through sensation. True genuine knowledge is to be achieved through the study of Forms and that study could ultimately provide a solution to an ancient metaphysical problem on whether mind independent entities referred to as universals exist.

How to describe a Universal? Think of something consistent and found wherever and whenever you look at it like the color red. Whether the particular distinct entity that you are looking at is a ruby or an apple separately or together they can both be red. Yes apples can be many colors but the most common apple is red as in a red apple for the teacher. That redness is the universal entity that is manifesting in both the apple and the ruby. Red is the common Universal. Plato felt that a distinct individual entity could only be identified by relating itself with a universal entity, in the case of a ruby, the entity red.

This student of Socrates agreed with his teacher's Form theories and also postulated the Theory of Knowledge as being a source that is genuine and unchanging. Consider there to be a constant bank of knowledge to draw on. Plato proposed something similar to Einstein's relativity theory that there is a constant that is unchanging. The constant has not been brought into being and is not destroyed. It is all one thing, all matter merely changes form. You can see where modern day theorists and metaphysicians got their basic theories around universal forms and universal knowledge. These very abstract philosophical issues are still studied at Universities today.

Aristotle (385–322 BC)
Aristotle was a Greek philosopher and scientist born in Stagirus, northern Greece. His writings cover many subjects, including physics, biology, zoology, metaphysics, logic, ethics, aesthetics, poetry, theatre, music, rhetoric, linguistics, politics and government and constitute the first comprehensive system of Western philosophy. There appears to be not much that he did not write about. The word philosophy itself originates from the Greek words philosophia, literally, "the love of wisdom"; philein, "to love" and Sophia, "wisdom".

Aristotle believed perception was the basis of all of peoples' concepts and of all of their knowledge. Somewhat along the line of what you perceive, you will receive. What is perception? It is something that you think.

THE ANSWER: THOUGHTS ARE THINGS

Great philosophers, great thinkers, deep thinkers, great wisdom seekers; all searching to explain mankind's existence, mankind's divinity, searching the earth, ocean and highest mountains.

There is basic learning from each of these ancient faiths and wisdom seekers. Can you imagine as Thales did that all the empty space around you contains all things? How about Plato stating that our world is a shadow of the real world? Write your thoughts below.

_____

_____

_____

Do you think that there is "genuine knowledge or universal form" that is unchanging? How would you try to connect with that Universal Form or draw on that Universal Knowledge? Have you had an apple lately? How would you describe the concept of "Red" being Red, no matter where in the world it was seen? Is it some special form of vibrating energy?

_____

_____

_____

Divinity lies within us all.

Over two thousand years ago, a man named Jesus found it. or learned it, or just had this knowledge and shared its secret. In the following of this holy man, somehow the secret of the divinity of man has remained well hidden. It is time for each of us to find that inner power and to realize our own potential to truly think for ourselves.

There is an era to consider and that is the era of the Æon Christ. The era was to restore harmony and heal the material world; this was to be accomplished by giving to man knowledge that would rescue him from the dominion of material matter and evil. It is not coincidental that Jesus became known as The Christ, or Jesus Christ.

I suggest that you open your mind to the possibility that Jesus was born with, may have discovered, was gifted with, or was told by the Great Omnipotent Deity how to seek the divinity and power with his conscious mind. With this known power, he was able to heal the ill, bring back eyesight, and raise the dead. But how did he do this? Did he use the power of thinking?

3.
SEEKING THE HOW

Step ahead to the new age thinking of the late 1800s, early 1900s, and 2000s. Authors started writing about the possibility that there was a "Thinking Substance" that, with concentrated thoughts, could be molded, as Wallace Wattles wrote in *The Science of Getting Rich*.

As a Man Thinketh, by James Allan; advocated that Man drew to himself whatever he was thinking. The *Law of Attraction*, by Michael J. Losier, declared that by creating strong thinking, vision boards, and vibration bubbles, mankind could attract to themselves abundance and health. *The Power of Positive Thinking* has long been followed by inspirational leaders of the world such as Stephen R. Covey; in his book *The 7 Habits of Highly Effective People*.

Reality. What is meant by reality? It refers to what you are living and find objectified in your life. Ralph Waldo Trine advocated that what you lived and acted out in your thought world would eventually be what you lived in your reality. Charles Fillmore's essay *The Real and the Unreal* (1906) [5].) delved into the nature of reality and advocated that there is a divine substance to be found in all things. Seekers for the kingdom of God need to have the knowledge and understanding that transcends the knowledge of the world.

> "We are told that matter has three dimensions, length, breadth and thickness; but we are also told that there is another interpenetrating quality called the fourth dimension. This physical science calls

> the universal ether, which pervades all matter, yet is totally unlike it. This universal ether is a postulate of scientists—they say it must exist as a foundation and cause of that appearance we call matter."

What Fillmore called ether we now know is the energy that surrounds and vibrates around us. Is this vibrating energy the "divine substance" that can be molded by our thoughts?

> "...physical science is nearly always forced to a metaphysical basis to account for its so-called facts. Heat, light, electricity, and in fact all the visible universe, are found to emanate from one vibratory energy. For example, heat is a vibratory motion in the Universal energy, or ether, and light is an undulating motion. Thus all the various appearances which we call matter in motion are but different modes of action in the one primal invisible and unknown cause, which we may call the Substance of Being."

> "...from the view-point of absolute truth that there is a universal Substance out of which these bodies of ours are formed, and that Substance is absolutely pure, perfect in every way."

How did Charles Fillmore reach this conclusion? He was a man of faith, but was he a scientist, too? He is writing about this subject in the late 1800s, early 1900s. What enlightenment did he have or what did he read or research to say that human bodies are of a pure and perfect Universal substance—and that substance is vibrating around us?

> "Through-knowledge of being, which is understanding-- we are to use it, and keep it. It is like the Substance, unlimited. That understanding would

> bring us into the consciousness of not only God with us, but God's kingdom within us."
>
> "Now this is that understanding and that wisdom which every one of us may have, that will reveal to us the truth of existence, and through that truth of that understanding we shall know how to direct and use this Substance, and harmonize its action in our organisms."
>
> "....the only lasting thing is the right use of your faculties, to properly form and shape through your consciousness, that Divine Substance—that Everywhere present Matter which is the source of all bodies, shapes and forms.
>
> When we understand, we will enter into the real, the real substance of everything; not only one thing, but everything."

He is saying that when we "understand", we will shape our world through our consciousness.

> "In our search for health and harmony, we have looked over the world and observed disease and sickness among men, and called it real. It is good for us to know that there is no reality in that condition. Back of it all is substantial health and harmony and a divine Law that is manifesting itself in perfection to the minds of those who will let it.
>
> ...the true thing back of it; because for every unreal there is a real, for every appearance there is a true Substance, and the knowledge is within. It is for us. Remember that. You can know; you can understand; it is not hard.

Jesus Christ demonstrated this law in a large way. Enter into the same place that I am and you shall know the benefits. You shall have this ability and mastery of the realm of possibilities.

…through the Jesus Christ consciousness… through the Jesus Christ power… all things in His name."

Fillmore's essay, like Wallace Wattles' book, speaks of a Thinking Substance, a Divine Thinking Substance that we can focus our thoughts into and attract power to us. It also touches on the possibilities of multiple realities as suggested by Dr. Travis Taylor, the Unreal and the Real, the physical senses, the metaphysical basis, and the universal realities. Is the vibrating motion of Universal Energy also a factor in these realities?

Albert Einstein imagined great inventions before they became reality. Einstein had a great expression: "Your imagination is the preview of your life's coming attractions." What is imagination? It is thinking.

What is your self-image? What is your purpose? Write down what you want to "imagine" as your reality for your life today.

_____
_____
_____

4.
SEEKING THE TEACHER

Let's step back to about 25 BC, and consider from that perspective the following:

Could it be that a young man by the name of Jesus performed his miracles by the methods described in the previous chapter? Prayer could be considered deep thought and controlled consciousness—and Jesus frequently prayed by himself. Did he practice a form of mindful meditation? Was he attracting to himself the Power within—asking for, believing, and receiving the Great Omnipotent Deity's gift that had been given to all mankind, but only known and used by a few? Even as a young child, Jesus had the power of the Word and was a teacher.

Speculate with me that Jesus' spoken word as recorded in the Bible is there to guide all who seek it to receive the Power to form our own lives. The Spoken Word of Jesus is found only in the New Testament, because of course he wasn't around in the time of the Old Testament. Check out the gospels of Mark, Matthew, Luke and John. Written there are His powerful thoughts.

How might we believe words passed down and written in the Bible? There was no internet or mass media in zero to 35 AD; there was no daily talk show called "The Life and Times of Jesus".

In today's age, if you read an article in the *Herald* newspaper in the western part of a country, then read a similar article in the *Journal* further north, then read on the same subject in the *Star* newspaper in the eastern part of the country, you will certainly get three different views. However, you would not dispute that the subject or event did indeed occur.

The same principle can be applied to the Bible, which is a collection of stories shared from the viewpoint of various apostles, disciples, and prophets as recorded in the New Testament; as well, the Old Testament writers recorded ancient myths and stories that were passed down through the centuries. Slight variations exist between the testaments of these people, but there is no doubt that there was a subject called Jesus.

He was not given the surname of Christ from his parents. Last names were not common at the time, so the couple Mary and Joseph were not known as Mr. and Mrs. Christ. Jesus was given his last name by his apostle, Peter: "You are the Christ," he said, as in the Æon Christ, the one mentioned earlier to come to save humanity from disorder in the material world and to give knowledge to rescue and protect mankind from the dominion of matter and evil.

As we are told by these historical recordings, this subject, Jesus, appeared to have a unique capability and tried to impart the knowledge of this capability to his apostles, disciples and more. He was driven to teach and heal at every opportunity, saying:

> ***"Verily, verily, I say unto you, He that believeth on me, the works that I do shall he do also; and greater works than these shall he do..."***
> —John 14:12

Clearly there was a Teacher, and there were miracles. And the time of Jesus was such an amazing time that literally the world clock was reset. (To this day, we speak of years as 2015 AD, meaning *Anno Domini* (in the Year of our Lord) referring to Jesus; any time before Christ is referred to as "BC". Some scholarly articles now use BCE, which means "Before Current Era", "Before Common Era" or "Before Christian Era".) This Teacher seemed to be totally committed to teaching mankind to seek knowledge and to have faith in their power. The Great Omnipotent or Omnipresent Deity was always close to Jesus; He was very happy with his work among mankind and declared:

> "And there came a voice from heaven, saying, Thou art my beloved Son, in whom I am well pleased."
> —Mark 1-11

> "For he received from God the Father honour and glory, when there came such a voice to him from the excellent glory, This is my beloved Son, in whom I am well pleased." —2 Peter 1:18

> "And this voice which came from heaven we heard, when we were with him in the holy mount."
> —2 Peter 1:19

Translations into English can contribute to the many paradoxes of the Bible. The word "this" in 2 Peter 1:19 in the original Greek or Hebrew is "taute" being a feminine pronoun which should be translated into English as "her"—meaning the verse should say, "And Her voice which came from heaven we heard, when we were with him on the holy mount." That is interesting isn't it?

Some early biblical writings portray the image of God as the "Forefather". The writing of Eugnostos the Blessed describes the main emanations of the perfect spiritual realm to be the Forefather, the Self-Father, the Immortal Androgynous Man, the Son of Man and the Saviour. These figures would be considered androgynous, meaning genderless.

Each would be "male" but would have their corresponding "female" portion usually called "Sophia", being "Wisdom". If we are strong in our faith, we could probably handle thinking of our all-powerful male Omnipresent God as having a strong feminine side, being that of powerful wisdom, powerful thinking.

A different light would be cast on many early Christian writings and scriptures and our interpretations if we could look up all the underlying Greek and Hebrew words.

Whatever translation difficulties there might be, it really matters not whether God is a he or she or all parent. God is God. A teacher Jesus who seems to be distinctly "he" was on our earthly planet over two thousand years ago. Jesus the teacher wanted mankind to rediscover some long lost skill, some long lost power, the capability to truly think for ourselves.

With this thinking for ourselves, mankind is to create what happens to us in our daily living, our daily reality and therefore be responsible and take responsibility for what we create and for what happens.

This is why again and again Jesus spoke the message of seeking knowledge, seek wisdom. He said we can do anything we truly think we want to do. Move a mountain; why would Jesus speak of such a large immovable object as something that could be moved. He was trying to get everyone to think big, think of awesome possibilities. Such momentous things could not be achieved by physically lifting the whole mountain and moving it. Nor did he want mankind to endure the back breaking labor of moving the mountain stone by stone. No, Jesus wanted humans to get back to using their brains, their thoughts and the power of God given when man was made in Gods' image. That is the "us" in the passage in Genesis. The "us" is the plural Gods that became the singular God.

> "Behold, the man is become as one of us."
> —Genesis 3:22

THE ANSWER: THOUGHTS ARE THINGS

Somehow we had the "us" power; somehow it was lost or taken away. If it was taken away, it seems that God has changed the all parent mind and wants to give the knowledge and power back. Jesus was sent to do that or at least try to do that.

> ***"I am come that they might have life, and that they might have it more abundantly."***
> —John 10:10

He was a powerful motivational speaker. He drove home his message with performing miracles by quieting his mind, asking and believing it to be done. Jesus said that you too could do this and by the way you are going to do even bigger things.

> ***"Greater things than these shall ye do."***
> —John 1:50

He came as the Christ to save humanity from disorder in the material world and to give knowledge to rescue and protect mankind from the dominion of matter and evil.

There is a Pathway in the spoken and written words of Jesus. We may have to re-translate the words written in the New Testament, strip away the parables and leave the meaning. That two thousand year old Pathway to seek the power of our own thinking brains is there. Let's all try to seek it.

5.
SEEKING THE LOST GOSPELS

In this "seeking", I feel that I have been "led" to find certain things; ideas have literally shown up in front of me.

My office downstairs has a small television connected to the satellite and television in the next room. Our eldest son was lounging on the chesterfield watching a program there. The show he was watching was talking about The Lost Gospels. My immediate thought was *What lost gospels? Aren't all the gospels in the regular bible?*

However, as I worked and watched, I learned that not all the gospels of the time of Jesus are in our Standard King James Version Bible. Some possibly very important gospels were left out by decision-makers for various reasons. Possibly these gospels didn't completely align with the Canonical Gospels that would promote religious institutions of the time. (Canonical Gospels is the name given to the Gospels that did make the cut.)

So with the great power of the internet, I searched out and printed a number of these "Lost Gospels". A lot of them had been found buried in Egypt. Discoveries of the Dead Sea Scrolls and the Gnostic Gospels of Nag Hammadi have brought to light more about the early days of Christianity.

Just like the Gospels that did make it into the standard Bible, the lost ones are prone to interpretation. A lot of what is in the Lost Gospels fully supports what is written in the canonical Gospels. Many of the statements corroborate exactly with the Gospels of Matthew, Mark, Luke and John; these four Gospels have been accepted as true descriptions of the life and times of Jesus. However, there are a few striking differences:

ASK, BELIEVE, & RECEIVE

From the Lost Gospel of the Apostle Peter (70-160 AD) comes the interpretation of some of the final words spoken by Jesus while he hung dying on the cross. The canonical interpretation that we have read all of our lives in the Bible has been:

And about the ninth hour Jesus cried with a loud voice, saying,

> *"Eli, Eli, lama sabachthani?"* (That is to say,
> *"My God, my God, why hast thou forsaken me?"*
> —Matthew 27:46

[Matthew's sentence is preserved in Aramaic]

And at the ninth hour, Jesus cried with a loud voice, saying,

> *"Eloi, Eloi, lama sabachthani?"*
> Which is also interpreted as *"My God, my God, why hast thou forsaken me?"*
> —Mark 15:34

> *"My God, my God, why hast thou forsaken me? Why art thou so far from helping me, and from the words of my roaring?"*
> —Psalm 22:1

Some of the manuscripts (the actual form of the Greek words in the text) give the translation of these words from Psalm 22:1 into the Hebrew:

> *"Eli, Eli, lama Zaphthanei."*

Here is yet another interpretation of the Jesus's spoken word (in Greek):

> *"Tee mou, qee mou, ina ti me egkatelipe."*

THE ANSWER: THOUGHTS ARE THINGS

The Lost Gospel of Peter preserves this saying in a Docetic (Cerinthian) form:

> **_"My power, my power, thou hast forsaken me!"_**
> —Peter: 5

Wow, that would put a whole other lean on it wouldn't it!

Jesus' words, **_"My power, My power"_** could imply that Jesus felt his power—the power to heal, the power to raise the dead—leaving Him. This alludes to the possibility that there is a "power" which is the power of God within all of us. The statement in the Lost Gospel of Peter supports the belief of an internal power, possibly an internal power in each of us. Is this the power of thinking?

Can you imagine the energy of a power within you? Where do you think you might feel it? In your heart? In your brain? Write some of your initial thoughts on this below.

_____
_____
_____

There are a number of gospels (besides the Gospel of Peter) that did not make the cut into the canonical Bible. Some major ones are the Gospel of Mary Magdalene, the Gospel of Thomas, the Gospel of Judas, and the Gospel of the Holy Twelve. There is also reference to the Gospel Book of Q, meaning *Quelle* or "source".

Followers called the Nazarenes used the Gospel of Peter for their teachings; this gospel was referred to by various bishops and historians in 190 AD, 235 AD, and 300 AD.

The existence of the gospel was recognized, but the actual gospel was lost until 1816 when the parchment codex was found during the excavation of a grave of a monk. Perhaps it missed the cut because it was truly "lost". Peter's Gospel has up to twenty-nine variations to the four Canonical Gospels. The first variation I have mentioned is about "my power, my power".

Another variation speaks to the event of the stone being rolled away from the tomb:

> And in the night in which the Lord's day was drawing on, as the soldiers kept guard two by two in a watch, there was a great voice in the heaven; and they saw the heavens opened, and two men descended with a great light and approach the tomb.
>
> And the stone that was put at the door rolled of itself and made way in part; and the tomb was opened, and both the young men entered in.
>
> —Peter 9

Who do you think these "two young men with the great light" were?

_____
_____
_____

> When therefore those soldiers saw it, they awakened the centurion and the elders, for they too were close by keeping guard. And as they declared what things they had seen, again they saw three men come forth from the tomb, and two of them supporting one, and a cross following them.

THE ANSWER: THOUGHTS ARE THINGS

> And the heads of the two reached to heaven, but the head of him who was led by them over passed the heavens. And they heard a voice from the heavens, saying, "*You have preached to them that sleep.*" And a response was heard from the cross, "*Yes*".
>
> —Peter 10

It is an interesting and enlightening scripture. The statement that caught my eye was, "You have preached to them that sleep." What does that mean? Could it mean that, despite the best efforts of the Teacher Jesus and saints and prophets prior to him, man of the time had still not discovered the power of thinking of which they were capable? Could the word "them" be reference to the inner soul that might be "sleeping" within each of us—not yet awakened to realize our potential to use our powerful brains to attract things to us?

What could you do to wake up your inner soul, your true potential?

_____
_____
_____

Some skeptics have discounted the Gospel of Peter, because a wooden cross can't speak. But the cross shape may have not been made of wood. It could have looked like a cross but was actually a mist-like formation of souls of the dead saints that were released (resurrected) at the time of Jesus' death. The rising of the saints and return to life is also spoken of in the Canonical Gospels which have been accepted by most as true reflections of the Christ ascension event.

> And the graves were opened; and many bodies of the saints which slept arose, and came out of the graves

after his resurrection, and went in to the holy city, and appeared unto many.

—Matthew 27:52-53

This passage says that some dead holy people returned to life and came out of their tombs, then went into Jerusalem, where many inhabitants of the city saw them. The King James translation refers to these resurrected people as "saints", which is why this event is sometimes called "the resurrection of the dead saints".

Another gospel with intriguing texts is the Gospel According to Apostle Thomas. It is a listing of 114 sayings written down with very few connecting statements to set the scenes. Many sayings match exactly the Canonical gospels of Matthew, Mark, Luke and John. All are intriguing. Here is a sample:

Gospel of Thomas (50-140 AD)

"These are the secret sayings that the living Jesus spoke and Didymos Judas Thomas recorded.

Saying 2: Jesus said, **"Those who seek should not stop seeking until they find. When they find, they will be disturbed.**

When they are disturbed, they will marvel, and will reign over all. [And after they have reigned they will rest.]"

Here is a clear and absolute statement that the Kingdom is within you and also all around you:

Saying 3. Jesus said, **"If your leaders say to you, 'Look, the (Father's) kingdom is in the sky,' then the birds of the sky will precede you. If they say to you, 'It is in the sea,' then the fish will precede you.**

> *Rather, the (Father's) kingdom is within you and it is outside you."*

Further statements tell us to understand that we are a child of God and to embrace that:

> *"When you know yourselves, then you will be known, and you will understand that you are children of the living Father. But if you do not know yourselves, then you live in poverty, and you are the poverty."*

Saying 92: **Jesus said, *"Seek and you will find"*.**

Saying 94: **Jesus said, *"One who seeks will find, and [for one who knocks] it will be opened."***

This Gospel of Thomas also advocates that Jesus told all to seek, and it will be found for you.

Saying 108: **Jesus said, *"Whoever drinks from my mouth will become like me; I myself shall become that person, and the hidden things will be revealed to him."***

Saying 113: **His disciples said to him, "When will the kingdom come?"**

> *"It will not come by watching for it. It will not be said, 'Look, here!' or 'Look, there!' Rather, the Father's kingdom is spread out upon the earth, and people don't see it."*

These are just a few of the passages written here as translated from the fragments of parchment.

The Gospel of Thomas states that if we can discover the meanings of these scriptures, we will not "taste death". It also states more than once to seek, and to not stop seeking until we find. Find what? Is it as stated above in saying 2? Let's look at that saying once more:

> **When they find, they will be disturbed.**
> **When they are disturbed, they will**
> **marvel, and will reign over all.**

Again, in these writings it is stated **"the kingdom is within you"**. Why would Jesus say that if it were not true?

Where within do you think the kingdom could be? Is the kingdom in the same place as your power is? In your heart? In your brain? Where? Write your impressions below.

_____
_____
_____

Here is one more of the Lost Doctrines of Christianity and that is the Gospel of the Holy Twelve (40-80 AD). This scripture is said to have been written very soon after the crucifixion of Jesus and may have originally been called the Gospel of the Nazarene—or it may have been the original Q (Quelle, "source") document on which the other Gospels were based, referring to material from it.

It does make sense that the apostles would have sensed the need to write down their collective memories to record the teachings and the work of Jesus, lest it be forgotten. One part of the Gospel of the Holy Twelve states that Jesus was not the "only begotten son" but that he was the "first begotten son". This would infer that Jesus was not an "only", and possibly not the only divine entity that chose to be human, but maybe a human that managed through persistent effort and faithfulness to "The Law" (perhaps over many lifetimes) to become a divine being. This is a Gnostic notion that anyone can also attain the same accomplishment.

The Gospel of the Holy Twelve declares that in order to achieve eternal life, "The Law" must be fully obeyed. This original true law is the "Law of Love and the unity of all life in the One-Family of the All-Parent".

Interesting thought isn't it? The Gospel infers that following this inner law is the key to salvation.

At this point, I offer a caution to you in your "search" for this Gospel; there are very few interpretations available for The Holy Twelve Gospel. The one that pops up the most on the web has a very heavy leaning toward "translating" the Gospel of the Holy Twelve to convince you that Jesus was a vegetarian, amongst other things.

This is not a bad thing. It is just that the effort is so heavy it takes away from other good thoughts that the Gospel could bring to the world today. To discredit the vegetarian claim: after the resurrection, and as Jesus appears to the Apostles, this scripture states:

> "And while they yet believed not for joy, and wondered, he said unto them, **'Have ye here any meat?'"**

Why would Jesus ask for meat if he was a vegetarian?

The law of love is also spoken of by Jesus.

> *Master, which is the great commandment in the law? Jesus said unto him,* **"Thou shalt love the Lord thy God with all thy heart, and with all thy soul, and with all thy mind. This the first and great commandment. And the second is like unto**

> ***it, Thou shalt love thy neighbour as thyself.***
> ***On these two commandments hang all the***
> ***law and the prophets."***
> —Matthew 22: 36-40

This sounds a lot like the One Law spoken of by the Gospel of the Holy Twelve:

> "Law of Love and the unity of all life in the One-Family of the All-Parent."

And the law written in Leviticus 19:18:

> "… but thou shalt love thy neighbour as thyself…"

Have you thought of the importance of love? What does "love thy neighbour as thyself" mean to you?

_____
_____
_____

6.
SEEKING THE POWER - PART I

Jesus gave instructions to the Twelve Apostles right before his crucifixion:

> *"But the Comforter, which is the Holy Ghost, whom the Father will send you in my Name."*
> *"He shall teach you all things, and bring all things to Your remembrance, whatsoever I have said unto you."*
> —John 14:26

This is clearly documented in Acts:

> And, being assembled together with *them*, commanded them that *"They should not depart from Jerusalem, but wait for the promise of the Father, which, saith he, ye have heard of me."*
> —Acts 1:4

> *"But ye shall receive power, after that the Holy Ghost is come upon you: and ye shall be witnesses unto me both in Jerusalem, and in all Judaea, and in Samaria, and unto the uttermost part of the earth".*
> —Acts 1:8

These are clear statements— you will be taught all things, brought all things to your remembrance and shall receive power. In this context could all things mean all knowledge? What type of power do you think Jesus is telling them they will receive?

_____

_____

_____

> Then returned they unto Jerusalem from the mount called Olivet, which is from Jerusalem a sabbath day's journey.
>
> —Acts 1:12
>
> And when they were come in, they went up into an upper room, where abode both Peter, and James, and John, and Andrew, Philip, and Thomas, Bartholomew, and Matthew, James *the son* of Alphaeus, and Simon Zelotes, and Judas *the brother* of James.
>
> —Acts 1:13
>
> These all continued with one accord in prayer and supplication, with the women, and Mary the mother of Jesus, and with his brethren.
>
> —Acts 1:14
>
> And in those days Peter stood up in the midst of the disciples, and said (the number of names together were about an hundred and twenty)
>
> —Acts 1:15

Can you put yourself in that upper room? You may have just witnessed the crucifixion of a great inspirational leader and now you are waiting as instructed to receive some form of power. What is going through your mind?

THE ANSWER: THOUGHTS ARE THINGS

> And when the day of Pentecost was fully come, they were all with one accord in one place.
>
> —Acts 2:1
>
> And suddenly there came a sound from heaven as of a rushing mighty wind, and it filled all the house where they were sitting.
>
> —Acts 2:2
>
> And there appeared unto them cloven tongues like as of fire, and it sat upon each of them.
>
> —Acts 2:3
>
> And they were all filled with the Holy Ghost, and began to speak with other tongues, as the Spirit gave them utterance.
>
> —Acts 2:4

Would receiving Holy Ghost have felt like an electric jolt to the brain? What exactly was this power? How would you feel if you could suddenly speak in many languages?

It makes sense that while the Apostles and disciples of Jesus were gathered and waiting for Pentecost that they could have written down their combined thoughts to be preserved as something called the Gospel of the Holy Twelve. Further separate New

Testament Gospels were written individually later, but this may have been the foundation for them all.

This scripture also implies that perhaps more than just the twelve Apostles received the Holy Ghost, the Power. It mentions more than one hundred and twenty, so that would have included followers, Disciples of Christ. So a number of things come out of this Gospel, one being that perhaps we all can receive the Holy Ghost, the Power, by divine intervention (Pentecost); or we can receive it by devoutly following the Law of Love and Unity of Life.

Biblical Writings in the three centuries after the death of Jesus

These "lost" gospels really should be included in the standard Bible and made more available for us all to read and decide what we want to believe. Appendix IV contains a list of some of the known Lost Gospels and Biblical Writings for you to research for yourself and come to your own conclusions. Remember that many are complex parables that cannot be taken "literally" but studied with deep thought to extract the hidden meaning and must consider effects of the translation to English.

The Bible describes a large amount of the history of man through its collection of ancient writings. As you view this listing of over two hundred biblical writings you have to wonder why more were not included in the Bible. Some of the gospels of the apostles who were very close to Jesus (such as that of Thomas, written between 50–160 AD, and that of Peter, written sometime between 70–160 AD) were not included. And why not include the "Sophia" of Jesus (50–200 AD)? Would it not have been good to read the "wisdom" of Jesus?

Early Christianity was not originally a major religious movement; followers were often persecuted until the conversion of

Constantine I the Great, ruler of the West Roman empire. This conversion started the process of making Christianity a state religion, and with the convening of the Council of Nicaea in 325 AD, to determine the relationship of the Son (Jesus) with the Father (God); then came the deletions and changes to the Biblical writings chosen to be in the Bible. The new political Christianity, became a sanctioned movement of the Romans and Constantine I. All these factors contributed to the destruction of the Library of Alexandria. This library probably housed a number of the biblical writings that didn't make it into the Bible, along with significant records of science, medicine and the arts.

Belief in Jesus became the cornerstone of the new state belief system. Biblical writings that did not follow this view (including subjects such as man's soul, spirit, and multi-dimensional nature) were rejected. The message of Jesus that all humans can achieve Christ Consciousness, that all humans are part of the Holy Spirit, was suppressed. This was in contrast to how Christians originally were exhorted to teach themselves and to be responsible for everything they did. With the now-limited biblical scripture, they were to only worship Jesus as the Saviour who would forgive them for the error of their ways and who died for their sins. They were not to try to achieve a higher enlightenment for themselves. If they sinned they could ask for forgiveness and be forgiven, which is good, but the seeking wisdom, seeking right thinking part was dropped. Thus Christianity was "Romanized" and became the official state religion by the Edict of Theodosius in 380 AD. The limited teachings of the Nicaea-influenced bible were used to suppress and hold power over the populace creating the dark ages of religion.

Those dark ages crushed pagan spiritual beliefs, other believers in the Lord known as Gnostic Christians and any other faith that was "different." Over time these dark ages passed, ancient practices that had been hidden were followed openly once more. Most faiths have grown and adapted with the growth and change on the planet, seeking the truth and becoming more accepting of others who follow different beliefs.

Unfortunately, in my opinion, there are still some religious leaders holding their followers in a time warp that is several thousand years old. Some faiths refuse to accept the progress of modern medicine to treat their illnesses, scientific revelations that prove that there is a universe of possibilities, the equality of females to males, and new knowledge now presented with the discovery of so many of these "lost" biblical writings. The least progressive economies are sometimes the ones where not every man, woman and child is allowed to equally contribute to their societies.

Very few churches (if any) speak to the human soul—what it is, for example, and how to achieve Christ Consciousness; nor do they teach how to communicate with our spirit, our soul, the God presence within each of us. I seem to have discovered by accident that at least part of the Answer appears to be in reading the words of Jesus. His words did not teach that we should kill others who do not think as we do—neither do they teach eye-for-an-eye justice, nor to believe that babies are born in sin, nor to fear God.

The words of Moses, Abraham and Jesus are to be followed by all mankind:

> Thou shalt love the Lord thou God with all thy heart, and with all thy soul, and with all thy strength: this is the first commandment. And the second is like, namely this; Thou shalt love thy neighbour as thyself. There is no other commandment greater than these.

Reading these "lost gospels" helped me to learn about Gnosticism (with *gnosis* meaning knowledge). The Gnostic Christians advocated that knowledge was the key to salvation as much or more than faith. This was not popular to the mainstream religious institutions of the time. Too much free minded thinking.

Gnostics were persecuted, and the gospels they followed were destroyed as much as possible. It's interesting that Gnostic Christians followed the teaching of some of the "lost gospels"; perhaps that is why they got lost.

Even the Canonical Gospels that did make it into the standard Bible support "knowledge":

> He [Jesus] told them, ***The secret of the kingdom of God has been given to you. But to those on the outside everything is said in parables so that they may be ever seeing but never perceiving, and ever hearing but never understanding; otherwise they might turn and be forgiven!***
> —Mark 4:11-12

> No, we speak of God's secret wisdom, a wisdom that has been hidden and that God destined for our glory before time began...
> —1 Corinthians 2:7

Now, didn't we read earlier about the Secret being hidden from mankind? Let's have a scavenger hunt and find this!

> So then, men ought to regard us as servants of Christ and as those *entrusted with the secret things* of God."
> —1 Corinthians 4:1

> Now to each one the manifestation of the Spirit is given for the common good. To one there is given through the Spirit the *message of wisdom*, to another

> the *message of knowledge* by means of the same Spirit, to another *faith* by the same Spirit, to another *gifts of healing* by that one Spirit, to another *miraculous powers*, to another prophecy, to another distinguishing between spirits, to another speaking in different kinds of tongues, and to still another the interpretation of tongues.
> —1 Corinthians 12:7–10

Could we find or be given miraculous powers?

> For this reason, since the day we heard about you, we have not stopped praying for you and asking God to *fill you with the knowledge* of his will through all spiritual wisdom and understanding.
> —Colossians 1:9

There are those words again: "secret", "knowledge", "healing" and "power"—written for mankind way back in 50–60 AD.

So are you convinced yet that the Bible and the gospels that didn't make the Bible seem to hold some directions, some encouragement to seek, find and use knowledge and thinking to enhance our lives?

How and where are you going to seek knowledge? Will you start by reading the scriptures in which Jesus is speaking? Write your thoughts down.

_____
_____
_____

Mankind was dealt a huge set back when only twenty seven gospels out of more than two hundred biblical writings were chosen for the authorized bible version. We might have harnessed our internal vibrating power generations ago instead of only recently becoming aware of the thinking possibilities that exist for us. The world might have been more peaceful with less warring over religious choices. It would be more peaceful right now if the one and greatest law of "love your neighbour as yourself" would be followed.

7.
SEEKING THE POWER - PART II

How do we capture this same Power that we, as Conscious beings who have eaten from the Tree of Knowledge, should have?

Do we have to believe that we are made in "His" image? Do we have to believe that we have hidden in the recesses of our brain the Power that the teacher Jesus had? You might first read *The Secret* by Rhonda Byrne. The book speaks to the power of attraction and suggests some good tools to envision things you may want in your life and therefore attract to you, whether that be health, wealth or happiness, a new car, a new home, or comfort of the spirit. It's a very good book, but why does this attraction work?

To explore this further, you might want to also read *The Science Behind the Secret*. Dr. Travis Taylor does a good job of explaining how wavelengths work and alludes to the complexities of the human brain. Two rocks dropped into the water cause rings of waves to expand, eventually intermingling with each other to create a new pattern. Light waves do something similar; they are light waves until they are observed, and then they become light particles.

Could we indeed have microprocessors in the cells within our brain, capable of sending brain waves (or thought waves) out—waves of energy to attract to us the form of what we want out of the Formless Substance that surrounds us, as suggested by Wallace Wattles? Is this Formless Substance, these light waves, actually the energy that Albert Einstein defined as the matter and energy that is never destroyed, only changing form? Is the Formless Substance the space of empty space described by the philosopher Thales?

Can we shape the light from a wave to a particle? Can we project our thought images into the empty space? Is this light, this space, the greatest thing because it contains all things?

The brain is a complex unit and has not yet been fully explored as to its capability. Recent research has shown that the brain does produce brain "waves". Thoughts are waves of energy. When these waves intersect with similar waves, they can cohere to each other and may more strongly attract other similar thoughts.

Every time we think a thought, an infinite number of possible outcomes or realities or dimensions are created. Metaphysics is a huge area of science and fascinating to consider. How do we best make use of the entirety of our brains as advanced apes, the created humans with a soul and with conscious and unconscious brain waves? Do we run on autopilot or can we guide or influence our life path? Should we look once more to the Bible? Is there something more to this pathway?

There is a leading line that is the motto of Newfoundland, Canada; *Quærite prime regnum Dei* (Seek ye first the Kingdom of God). It was originally granted with a Coat of Arms to the Newfoundland Colony January 1, 1638 by King Charles I of England. That same motto has been the theme used in some church hymns since the early 1700s, possibly before. The current version of the hymn "Seek Ye First the Kingdom of God", composed by Karen Lafferty, has combined the words of scripture with very inspirational music. This is a song based on scripture from the Canonical Gospels Matthew, Mark, and Luke and in Deuteronomy:

> ***Therefore I say unto you. What things soever ye desire, when ye pray, believe that ye receive them, and ye shall have them***
> —Mark 11:24

Seek ye first the kingdom of God
And His righteousness
And all these things shall be added unto you
Allelu, alleluia!

But seek ye first the kingdom of God, and his righteousness; and all these things shall be added unto you.
—Matthew 6:33 [4].)

Ask and it shall be given unto you
Seek and ye shall find
Knock and the door shall be opened unto you
Allelu, alleluia!

Ask, and it shall be given you, seek and ye shall find, knock and it shall be opened unto you.
— Matthew 7:7

For every one that asketh receiveth; and he that seeketh findeth; and to him that knocketh it shall be opened
—Luke 11:10

We do not live by bread alone
But by every word
That proceeds from the mouth of God
Allelu, alleluia!

The third hymn stanza uses scripture from the temptation of Jesus in the desert.

"It is written: Man shall not live by bread alone, but by every word that proceedeth out

of the mouth of God."
—Matthew 4:4 (See also Deut. 8:3)

Every line of this hymn song speaks straight to the three canonical scriptures. If you did nothing more than follow this song and these scriptures, you would have a huge handle on the answer to life and how to live it and be successful with your thinking. It is to be noted that every scripture used is a scripture that is thought to be the exact spoken words of Jesus.

These three Testaments all had the same theme with some stanzas written and solidified in song lyrics long before the modern version became popular. Prior to the written word being readily available stories and songs were used as a recording tool. These scriptures were considered as very important to remember and pass on. In this case not passed on as a story, but passed on in song. The Apostle Thomas's lost gospel also supported the previously mentioned testaments; "those who seek should not stop seeking until they find."

Let's dissect this. "Seek ye first the Kingdom." So the first instruction is to look for and presumably find the "Kingdom". Where is the Kingdom? What is the Kingdom?

I submit that the Kingdom could be considered the subconscious, possibly the super subconscious or universal mind, infinite knowledge level or the best reality/dimension there is. The Kingdom is around us and within us.

Could the super subconscious be a level of the "real world" where all the riches of heaven are ("riches" being the capability to form them from the formless substance, the energy mass of matter)? The Kingdom of Heaven has had much said about it. But how much has been a "religious" interpretation, and what is the true

THE ANSWER: THOUGHTS ARE THINGS

interpretation? Find the level of the Kingdom, the repository of all good things and God's righteousness; that should be our goal. This right thinking will see us through.

Jesus said, "***The Kingdom is within you***" and ***"also all around you."***

Is that where you have been looking for knowledge? Are you looking within you and around you? Where do you seek within you and around you? What are you thinking?

_____

_____

_____

Look at the Word "God" (sometimes referred to as Lord, Father, All Parent). What does this mean? Is it as it is referred to in this book as GOD, the Great Omnipotent Deity, or Great Omnipresent Deity? Is that why God knows your every thought—because God is within you?

Is God as Dr. Murphy refers to in his book, *The Power of the Subconscious Mind*, "Lord" "Subconscious" "Infinite Divinity"? The concept of GOD is more than a little confusing as there are so many references to God the Father, man being made in "His" image, God the Almighty, the Powerful to whom we are to turn, to whom we go for guidance, to whom we look for comfort.

How many interpretations of "God" have been given to us by religious leaders wanting to control their flock? Those first myths were very important to pass on, but the ancient originators could not have factored in that, over time, man or religious leaders would change or suppress some of the most important stories as was done with the limited choices of biblical gospels made in 325 AD, along with the attempted destruction of all others.

What is the real interpretation of the God word? The word God has been considered a noun—a father, a mother—but can "God" also be an action word? Could God, as a verb, mean "empower"?

God as a verb? Possibly an action word? Now that is a thought—God as an action word!

If you said you were going to "God" something, what do you think that could mean? Write that definition here.

_____
_____
_____

Researching the origin of the word *God*, I found that prior to when the Old Testament was put to text by the Hebrews, the words used for God were Ya, Yaw, Yah, Yahu, Yahweh, or El. Words such as Elohim or "Ehyeh asher Ehyeh" ("**I AM that I AM**"); are found in the Old Testament, the Hebrew word *Hayah* was also used (Exodus 3:14). The Hebrew word *Elohim*, which is translated as the word *God*, is actually the plural form of the word and literally means "Gods", as in a group of entities—not a singular one.

These names were used from the fourth to the first millennia BC. *Yahweh* may be a fusion of previous mythical gods and goddesses that had been worshiped by ancient peoples. The roots of Yahweh could be combined from *Baal* Zephon (having already absorbed Seth/Set); alternatives are Baal Hadad (Egyptian), Enki (Sumerian) and *Ea* (Enlil, Ellil) which is Akkadian and Babylonian. As these peoples in some cases lived in isolation from each other, different names were used to describe their guiding spirit. No mass media and connecting internet.

THE ANSWER: THOUGHTS ARE THINGS

The Hebrews, in the recording of their Old Testament, ascribed to Yahweh the borrowed achievements and epithets of the "gods" of ancient peoples' myths.

Later on, the word *Yahweh* had been changed by some to *Jehovah*. Searching the origin of the word *Yahweh* brought to me the unpronounceable tetragrammaton YHWH (Tetragrammaton means "four letters").

Some readings have indicated that the divine name *Ya* may have originally been an exclamation which then evolved to *Yahweh*, resembling the verb *hayah*. One-word nouns are common as divine names, but there is no parallel for a divine name as a bare verbal form. *Yahweh* and the verb "to be" are fused; the name means "the One Who causes to be (what is)," "He Who brings things to pass," or "the Performer of the Promise".

Imagine a crowd of ancient people shouting *Ya! Yahweh!* What could they be hoping to "cause to be"?

_____

_____

_____

Herbert B. Hoffman states that *Yahweh* is probably derived from hwy, "live"—be, become, to give life.

Further interpretations show the meaning of *yahwi* to be "to manifest (oneself)" or "to be present"; *ilum* means "god" as does *ilu*. This suggests that *yahwi-ilum* means "the god manifests (himself)" or "El manifests (himself)." The origin of the name may be from as far back as the 11th century BC. Can you imagine some really really early humans beseeching something to be present with them? To live?

Some interpretations have Yahweh's appearance to Abraham occurring in the Sinai, but further research would have the appearance being in Lower Mesopotamia, the city of Ur of The Chaldees. Chaldeans worshipped many gods; Abraham and Terah became aware there was only one GOD; monotheism began with Yahweh showing himself to Abraham and Terah in Chaldea. What was the image that they saw? However, the worship of one god was not understood or appreciated by the other Chaldeans who believed in many gods. This made staying in Chaldea difficult.

> Then Terah took his son Abram, his grandson Lot (his son Haran's child), and his daughter-in-law Sarai, and left Ur of the Chaldeans to go to the land of Canaan, but they stopped instead at the city of Haran and settled there.
> —Gen 11:31, *The Living Bible Paraphrased*.

> Then Terah took Abram his son, and Lot the son of Haran his son's son, and Sarai his daughter-in-law, his son Abram's wife; and they went forth with them from Ur of the Chaldees, to go into the land of Canaan; and they came unto Haran, and dwelt there.
> —Gen 11:31, *The Holy Bible, Authorized King James Version*

Two quotes from two different Bibles illustrate again how biblical text can be interpreted or translated differently. Some statements are written more clearly; in this case, *The Living Bible* tells us that Terah's daughter-in-law named Sarai came along, but the King James Version tells us a bit more detail indicating that the daughter-in-law was Terah's son Abram's wife. Despite this slight difference, both Bibles confirm that they went forth from Ur of

Chaldees—aiming for Canaan but settling in Haran—and that they left because they believed there was only one GOD.

A lot of the truth is in the Bible(s), but one must read with discernment, watch for parables, and be careful as to what is taken literally or figuratively. Parables were used to pass information on as there was little "writing" in ancient history (and few could interpret what little writing there was). A gift that structured religion of the early centuries after 1000 AD gave to humanity, was teaching the common people to read so that they too could read the Bible scripture. In the prior centuries to reach all people and keep the word alive, ballads, stories and parables were used.

Some of the myths alluded to previously have their origins in Ur of the Chaldees, preserved in found cuneiform clay tablets; archaeologists have also found a temple to *Ea* at Ur. *Ea*, mentioned earlier, refers to one of the gods that amalgamated to the One God. That One God spoke to children of Israel, descendants of Abraham:

> And God said unto Moses, I AM THAT I AM: and he said, Thus shalt thou say unto the children of Israel, I AM hath sent me unto you.
> —Exodus 3:14, King James Version

> And God said moreover unto Moses, Thus shalt thou say unto the children of Israel, The LORD GOD of your fathers, the God of Abraham, the God of Isaac, and the God of Jacob, hath sent me unto you: this *is* my name for ever, and this *is* my memorial unto all generations.
> —Exodus 3:15, King James Version

Here is our directive, then: "Call me God"; "I Am that I Am."

So yes, "God" could be a verb—the unpronounceable action word *YHWH* meaning *live; be; become; to give life*. It is also a very important word, remember that there is no parallel for a divine name as a bare verbal form. Further to this, "Jesus" is the Aramaic word Yeshua, a contraction of Yehoshuah, meaning "YHWH is salvation". To be, to live is salvation.

Is this the power that humankind is meant to have? To live, to be, and to attract that life to us?

Do you think God could be a verb (meaning an action word)? Circle one:

    Yes No Maybe

As stated in 1 Corinthians 2:7, God's secret wisdom has been hidden but is destined for our glory from before time began.

Another scripture to think about is "Seek ye first the kingdom of God and his righteousness." Matthew 6:33

"Righteousness" is a word that was hard to put a label to. Then the answer came to me through the book *Discover the Power Within* by Eric Butterfield. He said to use "right thinking" in place of "righteousness". It works. God's right thinking is what we should seek.

Eugnostos

It is interesting that *eugnostos* translates as "right thinking". (Word Domination.com) The Epistle of Eugnostos was known in 50 to 150 AD. Apparently it was not necessarily an actual letter written by someone named Eugnostos but perhaps is a written record of right thinking or righteousness that was important to preserve.

Early writings expressed their views concerning the origins of the divine realm. The writers appear to be preserving or expanding on the assumptions of the philosophers from 400 to 500 years earlier who elaborated on many things including the creation of the universe. The philosopher Plato speculated on the nature of the physical world and human beings.

Eugnostos the Blessed, sometimes called the Epistle of Eugnostos presents the insights of Plato into the one perfect and indescribable Good, called the God of Truth and the five main beings that emerged from that one perfect God of Truth or Forefather.

The Eugnostos writing speaks of the perfect spiritual realm of the Forefather and the beings or emanations that also constitute that perfect spiritual realm. There is the Self Father, the Immortal Androgynous Man, the Son of Man and the Saviour. As described in Eugnostos the Self Father and the Immortal Androgynous Man are firstly the mirror image of the Forefather with the Man being the emanation that emerges in the beam of light as the Forefather views his/her image.

It is interesting that again in the Eugnostos writing the Son of Man is described as the first begotten, not the only begotten. Here the Saviour as being revealed by the Son of Man as a great androgynous light. Let there be light is given importance in many writings, many scriptures. Light lifts the spirits and in some way connects us with the great androgynous light of the Saviour.

This Eugnostos writing appears to be describing the background of the spiritual realm that we should strive to be part of but does not give insight into who or how the material realm that we live in came to be and/or how we got to be here.

Is this some of the "right thinking" that we are to try to understand? Are we to know that in the beginning there was one and only one indescribable "Good", one Good of Truth?

We are to live with God's infinite empowerment of all powerful right thinking righteousness.

Should Eugnostus' righteousness be interpreted as God's empowerment of God's "nostus", "gnosis", or God's knowledge?

And so we have sought the Kingdom of Infinite Knowledge; we have set our course on Right Thinking; we have learned that we don't live on bread alone, but by every word that proceeds from the mouth of God. This is where we should rely on the spoken words of Jesus as being the Words, the Teachings that God meant to impart to human kind. There IS a path here to follow. There is an Answer. That Answer has something to do with the power of thoughts and thinking.

And now to ask, so that it is given unto you, how to knock so the door will open; or, said another way, seeking the door, having it open so that we may ask…

8.
SEEKING THE DOOR

Let's do a recap here:

Energy is neither created nor destroyed; it merely changes form. The earth and mankind was brought into being by a First Event, a First Cause. Whether started by evolution, or by creation, there was some power, some spark that started the first hint of life. That first hint of life also had to have the drive to survive and to thrive.

There had to be sufficient intelligence to meet each life-threatening danger with a power to change in order to surpass the danger—such as developing gills to breathe in water, developing lungs to breathe on land, and developing feathers to fly to escape danger on land. That spark was instilled into that first life, with an unlimited resource, an unlimited energy, an unlimited Life.

That unlimited resource, energy, life spark is still with each of us today. This dynamic force flows within us. The first force, the first cell of the first spark is still amongst us, because energy or matter has only changed its form throughout all millennia.

Once more, "Matter is neither created nor destroyed, it merely changes form." Start thinking about "how" that Matter changes form. Can we influence the change with our thinking?

Then said Jesus unto them again,

> *"Verily, verily I say unto you, I am the door of the sheep."*
> —John 10:7

> ***"I am the door: by me if any man enter in, he shall be saved, and shall go in and out, and find pasture."***
> —John 10:9
>
> ***"Verily, verily I say unto you, He that heareth my word, and believeth on him that sent me, hath everlasting life, and shall not come into condemnation; but is passed from death unto life. I am come that they might have life, and that they might have it more abundantly."***
> —John 10:10

Find the key messages: "I am the door", "hear my word," "believe in him that sent me," and "life" "abundantly."

We seek the door, having it open so we may ask. To believe in Him that sent me.

> **"Our Father, who Art in Heaven"** (possibly being the Heaven that is all around us and Father who is within us?) Our Father; him that sent me.

Christians believe in a triune God—the Father, the Son and the Holy Spirit. This idea of levels is the same belief found in ancient writings of India, that of Greek scholars, and in the religion of Egypt. The "Ka" was an ancient Egyptian's "higher self" that could separate from the body at will and perform any service requested of it.

How do we communicate with the triune God? Could it be that, "being created in His Image", each human is also a triune entity (the triune layers being the conscious physical body of an individual, communicating through their subconscious to the layer that is the super subconscious, the Universal Mind, the Divine Spirit, the Father, the Son and the Holy Spirit)?

THE ANSWER: THOUGHTS ARE THINGS

Is Heaven/the Kingdom actually in this energy level of the special inner super subconscious?

Is prayer "the way in"? The conscious part of our brains is a very minute part of it; a great deal of our mental functioning is at a subconscious level. Could we possibly train our conscious brain to direct our subconscious brain? The subconscious mind is a distinct entity managing all our body functions. Before brain development, subconscious intuition was all that animals had. They did not have the thinking power of humans.

The subconscious has perfect deductive reasoning; it perceives by intuition, and communicates telepathically, but it does not decide or command—hence the designation between "subject" or "subjective"; it is a follower, not a leader. The leader is you, through your conscious mind. Your conscious mind leads your subconscious. Through your thoughts, your subconscious just might be able to communicate with "him that sent me".

Can you visualize levels in your brain? Perhaps visualize the frontal section of your brain "talking" to a section deeper in your brain. Try it; close your eyes and think of a flow of thought going towards the back of your skull. Did you feel something inside there?

_____

_____

_____

The conscious mind is the connection to all the knowledge that you have gathered in your lifetime; it also is the connection to all wisdom and knowledge of past ages in the Universal Mind—the super subconscious. The ability to draw on that can give an individual access to all good things of life. Attaining control of your mind is attaining attraction to health, wealth and happiness.

Unlimited power is within the Universal Mind, the super subconscious, the Divine Mind. The Kingdom of Heaven is within you and can bring to you the life you envision.

But... the Subconscious can only react to stimulus it receives.

Albert Einstein said, "Imagination is everything. It is the preview of life's coming attractions." Why did Einstein make that comment? Is imagination the preview? Perhaps he knew that his thinking created his reality.

> The energy of the mind is the essence of Life
> —Aristotle

> All that we are is the result of what we have thought. The mind is everything. What we think we become.
> —Buddha

> Be careful how you think. Your life is shaped by your thoughts.
> —Proverbs 4:23

> As above, so below, As within, so without.
> —The Emerald Tablet, circa 3000 B.C.

> ***"Whatsoever ye shall ask in prayer, believing, ye shall receive."***
> —Matthew 21:22

> ***"What things so ever you desire, when ye pray, believe that ye receive them, and ye shall have them."***
> —Mark 11:24

These are but a few pervasive quotes that speak of thoughts, energy, asking, believing and receiving. Scientists, philosophers, leaders from long ago, all advocate the same line of thinking.

THE ANSWER: THOUGHTS ARE THINGS

Below are more lines from The Lord's Prayer:

"Hallowed be thy name…" (the name to call upon?). *Our Father, our inspiration, who art in the level of infinite knowledge, revered is your name.*

"Thy Kingdom come, Thy will be done…" *Thy era of infinite love, Love thy Neighbour as thy self; thy will be done as every word proceeds from you.*

"On Earth as it is in Heaven…" *In our inner and outer world, in our **reality** as it is where you "our Father" are.*

"In the beginning was the Word…" (John 1.1) In the beginning, God had the "Word", had "imagination". Was this Word, this imagination, the preview that created the first spark to create the first life? **"…And the Word was made flesh."** (John 1:14).

Is this the power of prayer? Is it actually the power of the Word? Is this why strong, focussed words of prayer can work? Words are formed by thoughts in our brain. That must be the source of the power?

Do you think the spoken and written words are tools? Do words have a useful power? Circle one:

        Yes   No   Maybe

Mental image, words, and strong conscious thought lead our inner spirit (subconscious) to connect with the Universal Mind, Divine Spirit (super subconscious) to create the Word into reality.

Have words or strong, focussed thought brought something into your reality? Write that thought here.

ASK, BELIEVE, & RECEIVE

Jesus prayed a great deal. Is this why he was able to perform so many miracles? Did all of his prayers end the same as when he raised Lazarus from the dead?

> ***"Then they took away the stone from the place where the dead was laid. And Jesus lifted up his eyes, and said, Father, I thank thee that thou hast heard me."***
> —John 11:41

> ***"And I knew that thou hearest me always, but because of the people which stand by I said it, that they may believe that thou hast sent me."***
> —John 11:42 (Here again is the reference to "believe that thou has sent me.")

> ***"Thou shalt see greater things than these…"***
> —John 1:50 (Is Jesus saying that we shall see and do even greater things than what he did? How is this possible?)

> ***"Because greater is he that is in you…"***
> —I John 4:4 (Did you catch the significance of this one?)

Are we supposed to realize that God, the Great "I Am", is in each of us right now? Greater is he that is in us.

Word and imagination is the key. Your own mind could be the creative principle of the universe. You need to have the knowledge and confidence that you have and you are the power. You

THE ANSWER: THOUGHTS ARE THINGS

must consider **Thought as being the Eternal Energy**. Is this "The Door" that we are to seek?

Have faith in your creative power, your unlimited power; the power is there.

ASK: With sincere desire, concentrate your thought on one thing, one Word, with singleness of purpose. Visualize; see yourself doing it, imagining the object in the same way that Universal Mind of God imagined all of creation.

BELIEVE: Have faith, believing that you have the thing you want, and that your vital force, your inner soul, is flowing through to create this reality.

Could you do something to convince your subconscious that you believe, and that you have received?

RECEIVE: Express gratitude for the thing you have received. Express gratitude for the power that enabled you to create the thing you received. Express gratitude for your unlimited supply of the vital force to create good things.

> *"Thank you Father for you have heard me...I know you always hear me..."*
> —John 11:41

Visualize a step towards success, just like an athlete would visualize a successful event. Hear, see, taste, smell your event, even though it hasn't happened. Can you adopt a champion attitude to success? What would you think and ask for right now if you believed you would receive it?

Next line in The Lord's Prayer is:

Give us this day our daily bread. Although we do not live on bread alone, we do need some daily thoughts to survive and keep the subconscious working and the conscious imagining. Perhaps "bread" is to be interpreted as thinking or Life. *Give us this day our daily Life.*

Jesus fed thousands on the mountainside from only a few fishes and a few loaves of bread. How? Did he Ask, Believe and therefore Receive? Did he invoke the Law of Attraction by blessing, saying "thank you" for the small quantities that he did have and "attracting" vibrating energy by thinking to multiply them into all that was needed?

Did he send out strong thought waves that cohere with the reality where there was plenty, bringing that reality to the people on the mountainside?

Authors of the late 1800s and early 1900s advocated that our mental attitude is the key driver for our life experiences, for the conditions happening to us. What we can do is only what we think we can do. What we can be is only what we think we can be. We can only have what we think we can have.

What we do, are, and have all depend upon what we think. We can never express anything that we do not first have in mind. Is this how Jesus provided the loaves of bread and fishes for thousands? Did he first think deeply of what was needed? As the baskets of food were passed around, they were never completely empty.

Jesus said, **"*I can of mine own self do nothing. The Father that is within me, He doeth the works.*"** There has to be faith and belief that the power of the Father is indeed within you.

THE ANSWER: THOUGHTS ARE THINGS

Powerful thoughts are built in our own mind, as are successful thoughts, happy thoughts of happiness and wealth. That is the secret of riches, of success, and of all power. Believe in this power and in your own belief in yourself. You can do anything you think you can. That dominant "Father" power within you is what attains things for you.

Jesus used that power from within and created food enough to feed the masses—food for all with loaves left over.

> *"If ye have faith as a grain of mustard seed, ye shall say unto this mountain, Remove hence to yonder place: and it shall remove; and nothing shall be impossible unto you."*
> —Matthew 17:20

Are we surrounded by energy, by matter that can be molded by our minds? Do we see what we want to see? Is what we see different to what the person next to us sees? Are we in shared realities, because we are sharing thought patterns with others?

> *"If though canst believe, all things are possible to him that believeth."*
> —Mark 9:23, 1 John 5:1

> *"If ye abide in me, and my words abide in you, ye shall ask what ye will, and it shall be done unto you"*
> John 15:7

> *Rather, the (Father's) kingdom is within you and it is outside you.*
> Gospel of Thomas:3

Prayer is a realization of the God power within you.
"The Kingdom of Heaven is within you."

ASK, BELIEVE, & RECEIVE

Think abundance, feel abundance, believe abundance, and abundance will manifest.

There must be a thought, a word, before it can manifest. Images are sent to the subconscious through prayer, by imaging the belief clearly on the deductive reasoning of your inner triune layers: **"Whatsoever it is that ye ask for, ye shall have it."**

When an idea or intuition comes to you, act on it. Joe Vitale, one of the participants in *The Secret* movie, suggests in the movie and in his book *The Key* that "the Universe likes speed." This is your Inner Mind prompting you on the path to achieve your Word.

Yours is the earth and the fullness within. **"*Nothing shall be impossible unto you.*"**

The conclusion here is that prayer is the way in. Let's not sugarcoat this by calling it deep meditation. Meditation is a huge asset in relaxing your body and mind, getting your brain in readiness, but then you must pray; you must ask.

If prayer is the way in, what would be your first ASK?

_____

_____

_____

9.
SEEKING THE WHY

How are prayers—"asks"—answered? Prayer is deep focused thought. Where are thoughts formed? Well, it is a safe bet that thoughts are formed in your brain, just as the ancient philosopher Pythagoras concluded. Exactly where could this be in the brain? Is there one specific spot? How are the sections of the brain connected? Different sections control different functions. There must be some communication network. The brain is your command unit.

Dr. Travis Taylor included in his book some findings of Dr. Stuart Hameroff. Dr. Hameroff has studied the brain and found that our brain cells have parts called microtubules that could have the same spin capability and electrical impulses that a quantum physics computer would have. Could this be our power centre from where thought waves are sent?

Standard digital computers "think" with binary sequential action. A quantum physics computer (if created) thinks in "all possible outcomes" at once. At one time, a human could complete the Rubik's cube challenge faster than a computer. Why? It is because the human brain can see more possibilities at once than a computer could. Now, with increased technology, the computer has caught up. The brain is not becoming more computer-like; it is the computer that is becoming more like a brain.

The human eye also "sees" all possibilities in one glance. Your eye does not send signals right to left, left to right, nor in an up-and-down pattern. The eye, in one glance, sends everything in a scene to your brain in one shot of coverage. This is a peripheral view covering the main screen, plus all the corners!

Eye exams often include the test where the optometrist checks your peripheral vision by having you press the clicker whenever you see a dot on the screen, no matter where it is. The eye takes in entire scenes, as does your brain; the brain records it for your memories and immediately programs all the possibilities for your reaction.

Why would we have such a complex eye if we did not also have a very complex brain capable of processing the information sent to it? The answer is that we have this complex brain so that we can experience all possibilities, all probabilities and all realities if we so choose!

The brain's subconscious part is your auto pilot that keeps things running in your body. Now, think of the possibility of commanding the conscious part of your brain to do something specific for you. You can choose to react positively or negatively to an event. Attitude drives the reaction. The event is 10% of the interaction, how you choose to react to it forms the 90%. Choose positively and command the brain to drop the rest.

Say you really want an event to occur for you. How would you command your brain to bring this event into reality?

_____

_____

_____

First, you have to have the "thought". You have to send the electrical impulse to focus your brain.

Send deep focused thought, thinking of one thing, asking, and "praying" for one thing. Send the word, this thought, regularly and steadily. Let's say you got the practice down pat and your brain is receiving a clear signal, a clear thought of what you would like to happen. Now it proceeds to "making" it happen.

Thoughts, brain waves, have been determined to behave like electrical impulses; could the impulse be "transmitted" out, seeking out other similar thoughts? Could the intense thinking pull what you had thought of and hoped for into your reality?

Do you believe brain waves seeking other brain waves could be the Law of Attraction? Circle one:

                Yes   No   Maybe

10.
FINDING AN ANSWER

Think about your life and things that have come to be that you had hoped for, had "thought" about. Write down how you want something to "play out" in the space provided below.

_____

_____

_____

How can you reinforce this success? Well, I suggest that you ask—pray—some more. Research performed by cognitive neuroscientists shows that repetitive thinking establishes a neural framework in our brains. Therefore, if we pray repeatedly, a direct and easy neural path, or a framework of wired connections, is made in our brain. This would suggest that if we want to draw on the power of our brain, praying is a good way to open the door. Perhaps it would even keep the door slightly open so that access would be easier each time we sought to be there. Jack Canfield's book, *Law of Attraction*, makes an illuminating statement: "Pray; it is the way in." He does not elaborate further—he simply states that "it is the way in." Interesting, isn't it?

Now, how to accentuate this Law of Attraction, this power of projecting and attracting electrical impulses with your thoughts?

A *Reader's Digest* article titled "How the New Science of Thank You can Change Your Life" by Deborah Norville hypothesized that "good feelings, generated by something as simple as an expression of appreciation, intervene in the release of dopamine, the chemical in the brain associated with happiness. The chemical is released when there is a feeling of excitement, of feeling good, activating the parts of the brain in which complex thinking and conflict resolution are thought to be headquartered."

Now, isn't that interesting: not everyone can express the emotion of love, even if they feel it. But most people can feel and express gratitude, thankfulness. This emotion accentuates your prayer to receive success from your focused thinking. It activates complex thinking.

Remember that thoughts are like electrical impulses or energy impulses; now add to this that emotions are like a magnet enhancing your vibration bubble. Now imagine harnessing this power combination. Magnetized thoughts are being sent into Universe to attract to you what you want.

Deep, thoughtful prayer with great thankfulness just might be how prayer works.

Rhonda Bryne, author of *The Secret*, hugely advocates the power of gratitude. And she is absolutely right. Think back to the Bible, all those parables forming a pathway to follow. It states quite clearly that God's first law is to love your neighbour as yourself. God was recommending the magnet of emotion all along.

The article on "The Science of Thank You" and the gratitude journal advocated in *The Secret* helps us look at life positively, to become interconnected, and enhances our self-esteem.

Eudemonia is a word that may be attributed to Aristotle. It refers to happiness and wellbeing resulting from an active life governed by reason. Various readings advocate that the action of gratitude helps to release that feeling of happiness and well-being. I love the way the Thank You article ends: "Gratitude has the potential to change everything from the ordinary state to being a gift. Now that is saying a lot."

THE ANSWER: THOUGHTS ARE THINGS

To recap:
The Bible appears to have tried to tell us that the path to enlightenment is achieved by following the words of the great prophets—in particular, the teacher Jesus who spoke of asking, believing, receiving, and of seeking knowledge and right thinking.

Wallace Wattles in the 1800s claimed that there was a "Thinking Substance" surrounding us, and that with deep and focused thought, it could bring to us the things that we thought about.

Could this thinking substance be the energy that Albert Einstein speaks of—the matter that is not created nor destroyed, but only changes form?

Could the thinking substance be the multiple realities that Dr. Travis Taylor feels may be created every time our thoughts interact and cohere to other like thoughts? The only way for thoughts to be sent out is from our brain. How does our brain do that? Does it truly perform like a quantum computer? Such a computer is a theoretical computation system that would be able to perform operations on data using phenomena such as superposition and entanglement.

Do you think your brain could be like a computer? Put another way, do computers "think" like the human brain? Circle one:

        Yes   No   Maybe

11.
TESTING THE ANSWER - PART I

I will share some of my own "asks"—prayers—that have been answered. Some of the examples come from before I knew what I was doing and why it can work.

I still had my accounting service at home when this happened, so this is quite a while back. A relative that is very close to me came to visit. We had played together as children but had not seen much of each other as adults.

He was concerned about a health issue. The doctor had told him that he may have cancer. Some tests had been done; results would be back in about two weeks. This news was very upsetting for us both. We talked about it and about other things and tried to remain positive.

Later that day I went to our church; it was midweek, so the sanctuary was empty. I sat down and I prayed. I prayed fervently. I prayed that the tests would determine that it was just some unusual infection that could be treated with antibiotics. I left it in God's hands.

The two weeks passed; my relative called me and said the results were back and that it was "just some unusual infection that could be treated with antibiotics". Imagine that—exactly what I had prayed for. I wept and gave thanks.

More recently, I was on a church committee with a small group that included a few folk from other local churches. One member was missing a number of meetings due to surgery. I called to inquire how she was doing. She said that while in hospital she had contracted several "superbug" infections. Her sutures were not healing and were oozing liquid. She was on an intravenous bag of antibiotics that she had to drive to hospital to get changed every other day.

She had been struggling with the pain and not healing for several weeks. The next day, she was going to see her doctor for the bi-weekly exam and to try to come up with another plan for treatment. We talked awhile, and when I got off the phone I went to my quiet spot and I prayed for June. Although her prognosis seemed bleak, I prayed that the results be the best possible outcome, and I left it in God's hands.

The next night, June phoned and was very happy. The doctor had removed the bandages and her sutures were all healed except one. She could go off the intravenous antibiotics to regular pills to fight the last infection. I was very happy for her. She laughed and said that she should have had me on the job sooner!

This event happened years before I had started researching the power of prayer. I was amazed that my prayer perhaps had added itself to the many prayers of others, influencing a positive outcome for someone that I did not know very well. We had only met a few times over the years.

Have you had a prayer answered? How did it make you feel?

_____

_____

_____

Around the time that I was starting to research prayer, my friend from the west coast was planning to travel through the mountains to Alberta to see her mother. This was mid-winter. I wrote in my

THE ANSWER: THOUGHTS ARE THINGS

journal that I hoped she would have a safe trip. Now, I'm not sure how well that worked, because she rolled her car on an icy mountain road! That said, although the car had rolled over twice, my friend was fine. She only had an injured shoulder.

We loaned her a truck to use while she helped her mother through hip surgery. She stayed in Alberta a number of months, and her husband brought her another car to use. In the spring, she wanted to drive her mother back to the west coast. It would have been a long drive on her own, so I offered to travel with her and fly back.

One thing that had upset her about the accident was the loss of a precious locket. I suggested that, on our way west, we take a detour and look for it at the crash site. She was excited at the prospect of maybe finding the locket but did not hold out much hope. I was deep into visualization at that time.

Before we left, I prayed that we find the locket, but I also sat quietly and focused on "seeing" the locket. The vision that came to me was of something shining in a small hollow with some foliage over the top. We drove through the mountains and stopped at the crash site.

There was debris and broken glass scattered all over; the ground was covered with a low mountain plant called kinnikinnick, which is only about six inches high, but spread all over the place.

I asked her to describe what happened. She said the car rolled twice and came to rest against some small shrubs. Those small shrubs kept the car from rolling once more and falling down an embankment onto a river that would have been covered with ice at the time of the accident. Maybe my prayer for a safe trip had saved her after all!

ASK, BELIEVE, & RECEIVE

We retraced the rolls. The car had a sunroof, so we could see where the glass had broken on the first roll and how other stuff had fallen out on the second roll. My friend went to look in another area, and I looked in a spot where I thought the car had stopped.

Goodness! Kinnikinnick everywhere! How on earth were we ever going to find one small locket in there? I crouched down with the sun shining from the east and focused on trying to find something glinting on the ground.

And then I saw that something "sparkling in a small hollow" under some fallen branches. Yes, it was the locket. My friend and her mother Pearl were very happy.

It is very exciting to find something that you thought was lost forever. Has this happened to you? What was it that you found?

_____

_____

_____

It seemed I was onto something—but why were only some prayers answered, and not all? What was making this work? What was keeping it from working in those times when the prayers were not answered?

The journal appeared to be a component; the deep thought was too, as was the prayer. Could it be that by thinking, writing, and saying a request I actually had "asked" three times?

It had always troubled me that a few people I really cared about drank alcohol and smoked cigarettes excessively. I was worried for their health and the well-being of those around them. Again, I wrote in my journal "asking" that they quit smoking and drinking for the sake of their families. This had been a lifelong pattern for them.

In separate incidents, both ended up hospitalized, which was very scary. But they survived. Neither one drinks or smokes excessively anymore. So although the path was rough, at least a partial success was achieved. There is only so much an external prayer can do. The "ask", the "thinking" has to come from within the person themselves, from their own brain, to be truly successful—hence the expression, "heal thyself".

That was just a taste of the successes I've had with prayer and with writing in my prayer journal. Each morning, I "intend" to have a good day, and in most cases, I do!

12.
TESTING THE ANSWER - PART II

HEALTH, WEALTH, HAPPINESS

Do not be afraid to ask for yourself. Use prayer, use visualization tools, use magnetism, use vibrational enhancing ideas such as observing, and resetting your vibes to be positive—but "ask" specifically.

Health

I've been blessed with pretty good health, but I've struggled with my weight all my life. I come from good, strong farm folk; we always ate lots and ate often. I was often described by others as a "solid girl"—and so I was as the years went on, slowly gaining more and more weight. I tried various ways to lose weight, rarely succeeding, and if so, not for long.

At about the same time as I made that trip through the mountains with my friend, I wrote in my journal these words: *I have a healthy slender body.* When I got home, I put up a picture of myself from about thirty years earlier when I looked pretty good. I did this after reading *The Secret* and decided to try some of the tools suggested in the book.

I have a healthy slender body was just one of many things that I had written in my journal. I did not dwell on it much. Shortly after, we celebrated our daughter's graduation as valedictorian of her college. As parents, we felt very proud, and there were lots of photos taken. They say the camera adds ten pounds, but once I saw the photos, I could have sworn it added thirty pounds! It was something of a reality check, because although I felt healthy and youthful, I was obviously quite a large woman in the eyes of the world and through the lens of the camera.

Not wanting to try any more fad diets, the idea came to me that I needed to work out. I faced the music and joined a workout group for women called "Inches Away". The name said it all for me. Three times a week we did leg raises, weights, stretches, and worked with many styles of exercise equipment.

Did I like doing this? No! Even the owner commented that I didn't seem happy to be there. "Of course I'm not happy that my body is in such a state that I have to force time into my life and pay money to put it through extreme paces just to get healthy again!" I said to Sue. Still, I stuck with it to get my money's worth. Yes, it was the money paid out that kept me there. One week, two weeks, three, four, five went by—then on week six, cha-ching! My metabolism was back! I was finally burning calories again instead of storing them. Five pounds of fat were gone, even though I hadn't really changed what I was eating except to add a daily homemade soup consisting of only vegetables and lots of them. It has a lot of bulk and fiber but few calories. Muscle equals metabolism. Why had this knowledge previously eluded me?

As it turns out, I stuck it out for the three months that I had paid for; I lost twelve pounds and twelve inches and they never came back. But what helped me to stick it out this time? I believe that writing *I have a healthy slender body* in my visualization journal gave me the boost and then events occurred to show me what I needed to do, but now how to keep it up? I could not afford all of the expensive machines that the workout group had and I could not continue to afford the money and time commitment that I had just gone through. It came to me that I really only needed one piece of equipment, a good resistance stepper to keep the longest muscles in the body, the leg muscles strong and the metabolism

THE ANSWER: THOUGHTS ARE THINGS

would stay strong also. That is why walking works for people who can fit it into their lifestyle. The key is to first get your mindset, your thoughts in gear.

Yet, it is hard. As soon as I get on the stepper I start thinking about how long before I'm done my 15 or 20 minutes and can get off of it. Then I discovered the technique called meditative or mindful walking that eases anxiety and rewires the body's response to stress by calming a part of the brain called the amygdala. Now I shut off the TV and focus on taking deep breaths and feeling them go slowly into my lungs. An advantage to being on a stepper instead of walking outside is that I can close my eyes while breathing to accentuate the meditation. Focusing on a positive idea (like losing weight) and meditative breathing increases the blood flow to the anterior cingulate and frontal lobes of your brain. The increased blood flow reduces the level of the stress hormone cortisol that interferes with the good metabolism revving hormones of leptin, ghrelin and testosterone

The anterior cingulate area of the brain can also be stimulated by meditative prayer walking, a mindful method of praying over homes, people, children that you pass as you walk.

Do you think these approaches—writing your vision for health and practicing meditative or prayer walking—can work for you? What would you try first?

_____

_____

_____

Allow me to share with you another instance of answered prayer: Someone close to me had been failing in health for over two years; all indications pointed to liver troubles even though there was nothing in his lifestyle that should have caused this. He had been hospitalized locally for five months with little improvement.

I had written in my journal on November 16, *Thank you for Paul's good health; his illness is all gone."* On December 24th I wrote, *Thank you that Paul is well enough to go home for Christmas. He receives his new liver right away. Thank you, thank you."* Later I found out that Paul had made it home for Christmas, but soon was once more in a hospital.

It had been confirmed that his only chance was to have a liver transplant and those could not be done at the local hospital where he had been for so many months. Yet it wasn't long before he was transferred. At least now he was in a hospital that could do transplants. I wrote in my journal as if a liver indeed had already arrived and was compatible.

> *March 31st*
>
> *Thank you, thank you for the healing presence that is right where Paul is at. Guide the doctor's hands to operate well as they give him a new liver. I project a vision of complete health for Paul.*
>
> *An image of wholeness, harmony and perfect health for Paul. The Infinite Healing Presence is with Paul, saturating his every cell, every atom with good health.*
>
> *A river of Peace and harmony flows through every cell of his body. I align myself with the Infinite Principle of love and life and I know and decree that harmony, health and peace are now being expressed in Paul's body. I am a Healer, a Savant and have the Power to Pray for myself and others. Thank you.*

But still no liver arrived, and worse, there was internal bleeding. Again I wrote in my journal:

> *April 4th*

> *Thank you for today, Thank you for all my days. Lord I ASK for a liver to become available for Paul today so that he can have a successful liver transplant right away.*
>
> *I BELIEVE that Paul can have a successful liver transplant and live to be healthy and whole.*
>
> *I RECEIVE the good news of Paul's transplant with happiness and gratitude. Thank you, Father, for you have heard me.*
>
> *April 6th*
>
> *Thank you for today; thank you for all my days. Thank you for the good news that I've learned, that Paul has rallied and is #1 on the North America list to receive a liver.*
>
> *Please, dear Lord, I ASK that the internal bleeding stop right now, that Paul remains healthy and alive to receive his new liver that is on its way.*
>
> *I BELIEVE in a whole and healthy Paul. I RECEIVE the good news of his transplant and good health with happiness and gratitude. My REALITY has a whole and healthy Paul with his family. Thank you, Father, for you have heard me.*

It was hard to keep asking the same thing again and again, but I kept it up.

> *April 7th*
>
> *Thank you for today, thank you for all my days. Please Lord, I ASK that I continue to have the Power to help and heal myself and others. I BELIEVE that I have already helped some to heal themselves.*
>
> *I RECEIVE this capability to help and heal with huge gratitude and thankfulness. Thank you, Father, for you have heard me. I know that you always hear me.*

But still there was no news of an available, compatible liver.

ASK, BELIEVE, & RECEIVE

April 20th

Thank you for today. Thank you for all my days. Lord, please, today, I ASK for good health, a sound and whole body for Paul.

I ASK that, even as I write, that a new liver has arrived at the hospital and has been transplanted into Paul. His surgeons are good and the transplant is successful. His tissues are healthy. He and his family are happy.

This I ASK. This I BELIEVE. This I RECEIVE with Gratitude.

Thank you, Father, for you have heard me, I know that you always hear me. In Jesus' name I pray.

That evening as I went to sleep, I visualized going into Paul's body and watching the old liver being taken out and a new one being put in, just as I had done on a number of previous nights. I also repeated to myself, *Live, Paul, live.*

The next morning, before going to church, I received a call informing me that a donated liver had arrived; part was going to a young child, and the remainder was being given to Paul. He was being operated on that very day.

Now, do you think that was an answer to prayer? I think so! I don't assume it was just my prayer, but perhaps my prayer was again added to many others and "tipped the barrel" over to a successful conclusion.

The answer was not immediate, but the prayer was constant, and I believe it created a stream of thoughts needed for a positive outcome.

If you are praying for health for yourself or for others, the use of visualization is very important. Joe Vitale, author of *The Key*, has written about quieting your mind and listening to what your body is trying to tell you about the pain or illness you feel. Vitale mentions the healing and enlightenment of using the ancient Ho'oponopono prayer from Hawaii:

> Divine Creator, father, mother, son as one... If I, my family, relatives and ancestors have offended you, your family, relatives, and ancestors in thoughts, words, deeds, and actions from the beginning of our creation to the present, we ask for your forgiveness.
>
> Let this cleanse, purify, release, cut all negative memories, blocks, energies and vibrations and transmute these unwanted energies to pure light... and it is done"

The Key also outlines a number of cleansing techniques, using gratitude to help find the source of the illness, asking your body what it wants you to do to be healed, and thanking your body for telling you. These are really good tools to have.

As you can see from my successful prayer examples, visualizing healing for loved ones may have helped some of them towards a successful outcome. However, it is far more powerful for the individuals to pray for themselves, to believe for themselves that they are healed or have received what is needed. Any prayers made on their behalf might jump-start the process, but may not hold up in the long term without positive thinking and focus on the part of the recipient.

Has this inspired you to ask for good health for yourself or for someone else? Do you think you could pray persistently and consistently for a good cause or to help someone that you cared for? Who or what would you ask for?

Wealth

Wealth-wise, I've had moderate success. Funds have flowed from unexpected sources and may have not come to me had I not thought, visualized, and asked for such in my journal and prayers.

Success, however, has come to me in my job. I was unemployed (and under-employed) for about a year. For most of my career, I commuted to the closest city. Commuting long hours had been part of each job. Having reached a certain level of maturity, I wondered if a lot of employers were averse to hiring "older" workers. How could I attract work to me? I realized that I had not been thinking of my ideal job or my ideal commute.

I wrote down my ideal job description: a position supervising a small team of accountants for a financially well-established company that paid well and treated their employees well. (My previous employer had run out of jobs, money and did not treat employees well). I wrote the ideal job description out a few times, refining it, and then left it. On my way to an interview, instead of driving to downtown, I deliberately chose to park my vehicle at a Park and Ride, and went on the Light Rail Transit. I visualized going to work each day, reading and relaxing.

I didn't get the job from that interview, but shortly afterwards, I did find employment with a huge, well-established company that was not afraid to hire older workers (the president was eighty). There I was, commuting by rail, with a small, hard-working team doing financial closes for the head office companies and subsidiaries of a multibillion dollar business.

THE ANSWER: THOUGHTS ARE THINGS

So why did I have success with this job out of all the other interviews? I believe that one barrier was a resistance inside of me that did not want to "drive" long hours to and from work anymore.

Subconsciously, this was holding me back. By visualizing an alternative by rail transit, that resistance dropped off. By visualizing my ideal job, with bonus, benefits and pension, that is what was eventually delivered to me.

If you are faced with a career that you are not happy with, or if you have lack of work, write down and ask for your ideal job conditions. See where that takes you. I think you will be pleasantly surprised with what shows up.

Write down what your ideal job would be:

_____

_____

_____

In editing this manuscript, I realized that a lot had happened in the wealth department since I first started writing. Going back to my hope/prayer journal, I had written a number of times about abundance and a big lottery win:

> *Feb 23*
>
> *I am so grateful for all the abundance that I have. The land all paid for, the $1,000,000 dollars of cash in the bank. I truly believed I would receive this and now it has arrived. Thank you, thank you, and thank you.*

Over that year, I had written similar statements in my journal and could not figure out why all this positive thinking was not yet achieving the abundance I had hoped for. Then a year later, instead of writing about a vague lottery win, I asked specifically for $500,000. Often we dream for way more than we may immediately need, or perhaps we are not specific enough. So I settled on an amount that I felt would clear off all liabilities, help family out, and have some left over.

> *July 1*
>
> *Thank you for today, thank for all my days. Infinite Intelligence, Creator God, I ASK for $500,000. I BELIEVE that $500,000 is a good amount to win or be given to me. Others win lotteries; others receive gifts of cash of $500,000, and I too can have $500,000. I RECEIVE $500,000 with joy and gratitude.*
>
> *This I ASK. This I BELIEVE. This I RECEIVE! Thank you, thank you, and thank you!*

I used Wallace Wattles' visualization technique of imagining, creating the money from the "thinking substance" that surrounds us. So I thought of small seeds growing in the ground, then becoming tall majestic trees on the mountainside. I imagined the paper being created from those trees, pulp formed, run into a printing press and $100 bills being run on a press, sheet after sheet.

Those sheets were being cut and stacked into bundles of $100 bills. Those bundles of bills were sent now, going to the bank account of the lottery association. Then there was the lottery association representative handing me a big cheque amounting to $500,000. There I was, holding that big cheque in front of me with a big grin on my face.

Still the lotto win was elusive. Recently it came to me that what we really should be asking for is for six winning numbers on one line on a ticket. It doesn't matter which lotto, the right six numbers or six out of seven numbers on one line in any draw could have a substantial reward. I look forward to hearing from Wendy our group ticket buyer to call and say that our group ticket is looking good.

THE ANSWER: THOUGHTS ARE THINGS

Funds can flow from many sources, not always by way of a ticket win. This year alone I received funds from unexpected sources. I had loaned funds to a friend many years ago and recently sent an email inquiring about the loan, asking that a payment plan over a year be considered: I did not expect a positive response. To my surprise she said that she too had been thinking about the loan and would pay me off in two payments within two months. It was actually paid in two weeks. Very nice!

We had also said goodbye to a close family member who had been hospitalized for quite some time. The lovely service was a nice closure to a long life. Later we learned that quite a sum of money had been accumulated over the years of her hospital stay and would be soon distributed to family members. Again, funds were going to be coming from an unexpected source.

Have you been pleasantly surprised by unexpected funds arriving? If not, can you imagine exactly that happening? How do you want money to arrive?

_____
_____
_____

Wealth can be influenced by your own thinking and your own decisions. A friend gave me a book called *The Secrets of the Millionaire Mind*. Author T. Harv Eker talks about how we are often conditioned by our upbringing or past events to put down and basically repel money by our negative thoughts about wealth.

To turn this around, we are to revisit our past thoughts about money and only keep the views that empower ourselves. At each chapter's end, Eker asks you to touch your head and say, "I have a millionaire mind." For those that would put down the idea of "thinking" of wealth, they might not be thinking realistically. We were never meant to live in poverty.

Wealth has built the churches that are worshipped in, even since biblical times; wealth is what enables missions and gets help to those in need. Wealth is not a bad thing. We admire our philanthropists. Start planning on becoming one, giving away money to good purposes.

Eker also writes of "cause and effect". The cause quadrants are the worlds of emotion, mental force and spiritual force. The effect is the physical world, and it is a world brought on by the three effects of emotional, mental and spiritual causes. Your inner world creates your outer world. He calls it the printout of what you were thinking.

Earn your money through "purpose, contribution and joy". Commit yourself to being wealthy, commit yourself to emulating wealthy people, and try to think like a wealthy person. Commit yourself to finding your value in the marketplace, bless what you want, adopt a mindset of champions.

Say to yourself that you are worthy and that you are worthy of more. Do not live in a world of limitations; live in a world of abundance. Practical advice from this book is to focus on your net worth and working income versus passive income. Savings are imperative; allocate ten percent of every dollar of working income received to savings to be used to earn passive income.

Eker states that you are to train and manage your mind, your consciousness. Choose and focus on empowering thoughts; this is power thinking. Knowledge is power and power is the ability to act. Love financial freedom; just think how much you can donate to your chosen cause.

What cause would you donate to? Can you visualize handing over the cheque?

_____
_____
_____

Happiness

Happiness is attainable by most of us. It might take toning down the expectations a bit and not letting adversity get you down. When you suffer a setback, try to find a positive in the situation. Sometimes, being in a traffic jam means that you weren't the one in the accident that you eventually inch your way past.

I had lost a pretty high-level job at one time due to downsizing. It was pretty devastating, not to mention bad timing as our eldest had just started university. However, when fellow employees were shocked and upset on my behalf, I said to them, "It's okay—nobody died. I just lost my job." At least I was still on this side of the grass, able to fight the good fight.

Fortunately, I got a decent enough severance package and was working again within two weeks, partly due to the fact that I did not let the loss get me down. Looking back, I see now that the position I lost had been harmful to my health, and that I needed to move on. I just got moved sooner than I was ready for!

"Why do bad things still happen to good people?"

Despite the best focusing and the best praying that can be managed, the unimaginable can happen. It is a real bitter pill to swallow when an illness, a death, or a tragedy occurs. This type of event should not occur because this is not at all what your thoughts have ever focused on.

In some cases, it may be as it was for the man Job in the Bible:

> And the LORD said, Hast thou considered my servant Job, that there is none like him in the earth, a perfect and an upright man, one that feareth God, and escheweth evil?
> —Job 1:8

And yet Job had troubles, had afflictions. Job said, "What I have thought has come upon me."

Sometimes our innermost fears, though we may think we keep them hidden, have set in motion the attraction of something we don't want to come our way. It takes a strong mind and a strong heart to pull away from negative thinking and focus only on positive things.

Unfortunately, I again experienced a loss of employment and was in shock at how it happened, when it happened, why it happened, and the effect it had on me and on my staff. This was not something that I was "thinking" about… was it?

Despite positive thinking, focus, and praying, it still happened. I was handed my packed up proverbial box of personal stuff, got my taxi chit, and took my stressed body home.

Once home—after unemployment benefits were applied for, and after a few phone calls—I had time to reflect. I realized that yes; I had brought this upon myself. Events at work had brought to the surface that our group feared the internal auditors, feared the external auditors, and feared the financial reporting group because our accounting work was constantly reviewed and critiqued and criticized by all these. We often cringed at the demeaning and demanding tone of the emails and interactions with financial reporting.

THE ANSWER: THOUGHTS ARE THINGS

One employee in my group refused to share the workload of another, despite a thorough review that proved the work load was terribly imbalanced. The work days had an underlying layer of constant stress from trying to encourage that one employee to shed her aura of entitlement, her constant socialization, and to be productive at work. I lay awake at night for months trying to figure out ways to gently encourage her. I asked someone in human resources to help me. She agreed that there was a problem but refused to help.

A conflict arose between the two staff and this brought interaction with the company human resources department. Their review was very secretive, very restricted, with huge confidentiality, and yet did not encompass a review of the staff emails. The emails could reveal the truth one way or the other. For suggesting an email review I was severely criticized and received a letter of reprimand that I was favouring one staff member over the other. What I had really needed was help to manage the one employee, to encourage her to help the other employee.

This help I had requested of the human resources department on three different occasions prior to the conflict and had been refused each time. In all my years of managing teams I had always stuck up for my staff and had the support of human resources departments. Now I needed someone to help defend me from lies, and no one was there for me—least of all my boss. He had no belief in his staff. He did whatever human resources told him to do.

That is when the first twinge of fear of loss of job arose. One of the staff found another job within the group of companies, was all signed up, and was very grateful, looking forward to a change. Then shock of shocks, the corporate human resources department forced the subsidiary to withdraw the offer. Devastating to the single mother of two young girls, she suffered a complete breakdown and went on disability leave. Further to this, the human resources department and their insurance agency denied her disability claim even though she had a valid doctor's note proving her inability to return to work.

On my part, disbelief, the realization that this human resources department was neither human nor resourceful, how could they do this to another human being that was hoping to make a fresh start somewhere new? Because I had made the initial suggestion that she apply for this new job, I was again deemed to be favouring this staff person. I then realized that my personal values were very different from the hurtful values that I was seeing at this company.

Once more, I felt fear of job loss, and yet I was a strong team leader and had brought a lot of positive, productive change to our group and to the strength and accuracy of the corporate financial statements. Work had been completed that had been left undone for years. Period ends and year-ends were now done on time without overtime.

Despite trying to suppress the fear, I see now that it was always there in the background. I had anxiety attacks any time someone from human resources or the corporate communications department came on our floor. Added to this was the lack of sleep for two years from stress. The fear of loss of job was there just hidden deep within me. But why would this draw to me exactly what I did not want? Again, I had a light bulb of insight!

Fear is an emotion—a deep emotion, a strong emotion, a primal emotion for all creatures. Survival requires immediate reaction to fear. Delay could be fatal. This emotion for humans strikes at the deepest subconscious level. No wonder my subconscious, my brain, had attracted this to me. I had "feared" my way out of a job.

How to counter a scenario like this?

Express Love. Follow the ancient guideline: "And the greatest of these is love." Strive to love thy neighbours—and yes, love "thine" enemies as much as you possibly can. A response to my work situation could be reframed like this:

> *Thank you, thank you that I am away from the stress. Thank you, thank you that this event happened so that I might understand the importance of keeping love at the forefront of my thoughts, my mind, my soul; thank you for reminding me of the importance of keeping true to my own values.*

I believe in a forgiving God. In the case of this company that had so recently hurt me, I think God might make an exception and not be quite so forgiving of the evil acts done to employees by the human resources department. Yet I myself will try to forgive and to forget the pain. Perhaps guiding angels moved me so quickly to save me from more attacks, more anguish. And perhaps someday the owner of the company will realize that her corporate human resources department is stifling management decisions and affecting her company and subsidiaries in a manner detrimental to the heart and mind of the firm first established years ago.

I do occasionally visualize great bright orbs of angel lights flowing through that human resources department floor, clearing out all the evil. It has a cleansing effect on the soul. Ironically, the productivity and socialization issues were all worked out, prior to my leaving, by an outsourced mediation effort. Perhaps a facilitator should have been provided when I first requested it over a year earlier.

There surely are guiding angels, for I was at ease again by the next week. Further to this, as I worked at forgiving, I visualized delivering bouquets of flowers to those who had hurt me, with a note saying, "Father, forgive them, they know not what they do." Something must have clicked, because all my stress and sadness melted away. I soon had a new career path, along with going into partnership on a business, managing to finish this book, and have tripled my income from what I was earning as an employee.

The angel orbs did flow through that company clearing out many staff. Thank you, Thank you, and Thank you. Have you suffered a job loss? How did you cope? Do you think visualizing bright, glowing, powerful orbs helping you would make you feel better?

_____

_____

_____

Without focused thinking, life can still be good, but more probably by chance. Your brain, your conscious mind, your subconscious will run only on autopilot. Survival mode is in effect only; and not necessarily in thriving mode. Not trying to control your thoughts or to focus your life leaves you open to being drawn into someone else's reality.

Their reality might not be favourable to you. The autopilot mode also leaves you exposed to very unhappy and unkind people's thoughts. Yes, there are not-as-nice folk out there who seem to want to deliberately hurt others. Perhaps they have been hurt themselves.

It is hard when you are attacked by others, especially in an environment where you had previously felt safe or by someone that you had previously trusted. You may have also thought that you had your back covered by someone you expected to support you, defend you. Don't trust your boss or the person that hired you to stick up for you; it didn't work for me.

THE ANSWER: THOUGHTS ARE THINGS

There is evil in the world. I like to believe that love is stronger. In one of my readings, it was said that "Yes, there is evil, but it is only here in the tiniest trace amounts. Evil was necessary, because without it, free will was impossible, and without free will there could be no growth—no forward movement, no chance for us to become what God longed for us to be." [6].)

It is better to be in control of your reality to keep the not-nice thoughts out of your life, out of your vibration bubble, and out of your reality if you can. There is a better chance of this being successful if you have your brain constantly planning positive outcomes for you. There is also that one line that you may be "asking" each day through prayer:

"But deliver us from evil".

Still, how do you cope with the stress, and where do you seek guidance? Some successful tools come from Napoleon Hill's book *Think and Grow Rich*. He spoke of striving to develop a sixth sense to connect the finite mind with infinite intelligence. It is the sixth sense that is there to warn you of impending dangers in time to avoid them. It is intuition, inspiration—a guardian angel to do your bidding, to draw a power to you and, when needed, to protect you. Imagine feeling enveloped in a protective shell or sheltered by large angel wings. It could go a long way towards easing your stress.

Napoleon Hill also created a mental group of "Invisible Counsellors" for himself. Hill used this group as mentors to emulate. His chosen group included men whose lives and life work he admired. Hill endeavoured to reshape his character from traits he saw in leaders of his time, such as Emerson, Edison, Lincoln, Ford, and Carnegie.

Don't Worry, Be Happy! Draw your guardian angels to yourself; create your own group of Invisible Counsellors. Yes, it is pretend, and use whatever tools necessary to bring you back to the positives of life, and to enlightenment.

13.
SEEKING OTHER SEEKERS

Seekers in the Previous Century

Remember how I had given a colleague of mine some ideas for the type of books that I was reading or was going to read? Well, I just recently purchased one of the "yet-to-read" books. The title intrigued me.

Thoughts Are Things – Prentice Mulford 1834–1891

I had to order it in as most books that are over 100 years old are not sitting on the bookstore shelf. It came as *Thoughts are Things & the Real and the Unreal: The Collected "New Thought" Wisdom of Prentice Mulford and Charles Fillmore.*

These men were two "seekers" from the late 1800s.

Prentice Mulford understood long ago that "thoughts are things". He really didn't have all the mechanics on how thoughts brought things to the thinker, but he painted a pretty good picture in this book.

Full credit goes Mr. Mulford for being such a wise and forward thinking man. Look at the chapter titles; these were meant to inspire the reader of his time and to still inspire us today: Can you imagine it being bought by people from a travelling merchant selling his wares from a wagon being pulled by horses? Would you be drawn to read it?

Chapter One - THE MATERIAL MIND V. THE SPIRITUAL MIND

Chapter Three - THOUGHT CURRENTS

Chapter Four - ONE WAY TO CULTIVATE COURAGE.

Chapter Five - LOOK FORWARD

Chapter Six - GOD IN THE TREES; OR, THE INFINITE MIND OF NATURE.

Chapter Seven - SOME LAWS OF HEALTH AND BEAUTY

Chapter Nine - THE GOD IN YOURSELF

Chapter Ten - THE HEALING AND RENEWING FORCE OF SPRING

Chapter Eleven - IMMORTALITY IN THE FLESH

Chapter Twelve - THE ATTRACTION OF ASPIRATION

Chapter Thirteen - THE ACCESSION OF NEW THOUGHT

Chapters Two and Eight aren't mentioned as they seemed out of sync with the rest of his book. Can you imagine being a pioneer struggling to survive in a new land and reading this book about all the possibilities of a new life being formed by their own thoughts? It was reading this book that inspired me to realize that thoughts indeed are things. This is why focused thoughts work; they are real things being transmitted.

Overall the foresight of Mulford is amazing and the following elaborates on five of the chapters.

Chapter One- THE MATERIAL MIND V. THE SPIRITUAL MIND

In Chapter I, Mulford is setting the stage that there are two parts to the brain, giving many contrasting statements of what he called the Spiritual Mind (Higher Self) and Material Mind (Lower Self). He describes the Material Mind as accepting life as it comes,

THE ANSWER: THOUGHTS ARE THINGS

not believing there is more and the Spiritual Mind as rising up to Believe and Achieve more.

The description is somewhat in line with what is also referred to as the Subconscious Mind and Conscious Mind. How many of us are locked into the mode of Material Mind, just accepting the life we are living even though it may not be a happy rewarding life?

> THERE belongs to every human being a higher self and a lower self or mind of the spirit which has been growing for ages, and a self of the body, which is but a thing of yesterday. The higher self is full of prompting idea, suggestion and aspiration. This it receives of the Supreme Power...The higher self argues possibilities and power for us greater than men and women now possess and enjoy...

> The higher self-craves freedom from the cumbrousness, the limitations, the pains and disabilities of the body....The higher self wants a standard for right and wrong of its own. The lower self says we must accept a standard made for us by others--by general and long-held opinion, belief and prejudice...

He talks of telepathic communication:

> The spiritual mind will know that your thought influences people for or against your interests, though their bodies are thousands of miles distant.

> The spiritual mind knows that every one of its thousand daily secret thoughts is a real thing acting on the minds of the persons they are sent to.

He speaks of matter being created from thought:

> The spiritual mind knows that matter or the material is only an expression of spirit or force; that such

matter is ever changing in accordance with the spirit that makes or externalizes itself in the form we call matter.

To Say a thing must be; it is the very power that makes it.

What do you think of that statement? Saying something is the power that will make it happen.

What would you say and have happen?

_____

_____

_____

Mulford inspires us with these words:

> …when the spiritual mind has once commenced to awaken; nothing can stop its further waking.
>
> Then all power can be given to your spirit. Then all such force will be used to further undertakings, to bring us material goods, to raise us higher and higher into realms of power, peace and happiness, to accomplish what now would be called miracles.
>
> Life becomes then one glorious advance forward from the pleasure of today to the greater pleasure of tomorrow, and the phrase "to live" means "to enjoy."

Chapter Three - THOUGHT CURRENTS

Thoughts are currents. All of us have thought currents flowing to and from us constantly. (This vibration bubble or cloud around each of us is also spoken of by current-century author Michael J. Losier in his book *Law of Attraction.*)

THE ANSWER: THOUGHTS ARE THINGS

The next time you are sitting on a bus or in a group of people, think of the air being full of thoughts with each person having a luminous cloud above them—something like a cartoon balloon. Surely in all those bubbles and balloons full of thought impulses there are a few that are similar to one another.

Visualize those similar thought currents joining together into one person's bubble. As that person's bubble goes through the day, his or her bubble more strongly attracts other similar thoughts from other thought currents.

Now think of the internet and how in mere seconds or less, information can be retrieved from all around the world. Could not our own thought currents do the same? Could they too retrieve and attract other thought currents from around the globe?

Mulford touches on universal human consciousness in this chapter.

> "A fanatic predicts a catastrophe."

The more minds, and therefore the more thought currents that pick up the media attention, the more escalated and more the possibility of the event becomes. The news media can be a vulture for bad and sensational news. It would be great if in each newscast, there was a mandate for nothing but positive coverage on uplifting events.

Mulford is on track in telling us to keep as positive as we can be, and to "demand the highest good", for there is no limit to the power of the thought current you can attract.

> We need to be careful of what we think and talk; because thought runs in currents as real as those of air and water. Of what we think and talk we attract to us like current of thought. This acts on mind or body for good or ill.

> If thought was visible to the physical eye we should see its currents flowing to and from people. We should see that persons similar in temperament, character and motive are in the same literal current of thought.

Visualize thought currents flowing to and from you. What is in your thought bubble? Write down what you would want these currents to attract to you.

_____

_____

_____

Mulford also talks of common thoughts acting like a generator and boosting the thought into reality.

> ...and that each one in such moods; serves as an additional battery or generator of such thought; and is strengthening that particular element. We should see these forces working in similar manner and connecting the hopeful, courageous and cheerful, with all others hopeful, courageous and cheerful.

This supports the principle set forth in Matthew 18:19:

> ***Again I say unto you, that if two of you shall agree on earth as touching any thing that they shall ask, it shall be done for them of my Father which is in heaven."***

Here is Mulford's version of the Bible's "two or more gathered in His Name"

> If but two people were to meet at regular intervals and talk of health, strength and vigour of body and mind, at the same time opening their minds to receive of the Supreme the best idea as to the ways

THE ANSWER: THOUGHTS ARE THINGS

> and means for securing these blessings, they would attract to them a thought current of such idea.

The human consciousness —is it a vibrant collective of thought? Are there world-wide trends caused by "group" thinking? Have some of the worst and best world events been brought on by human thought? Should we try to constantly think of world peace?

> A fanatic predicts a great catastrophe. The sensational newspapers take up the topic, ventilate it, and affect to ridicule but still write about it. This sets more minds to thinking and more people to talking. The more talk, the more of this injurious force is generated.
>
> As a result, thousands of people are affected by it unpleasantly, some in one way, some in another, because the whole force of that volume of fear is let loose upon them.

Group consciousness and its possible effects are currently being studied by modern era researchers such as Dr. Hameroff. Is it possible that today's minute-by-minute media coverage piped into our homes can actually escalate an already bad event? Circle one:

        Yes   No   Maybe

Mulford speaks of personal power, how it can grow to your benefit:

> Your power increases to bring results. You are wonderstruck at the fact that when your mind is set in the right direction all material things come to you with very little physical external effort...

> You will see in this demand for the highest good that you are growing to power greater than you ever dreamed of...

> You find as you get more and more into the current of the Infinite Mind... all things needful will come to you...

> There is no limit to the power of the thought current you can attract to you nor limit to the things that can be done through the individual by it.

Is this truly the "Time of Miracles" once more?

> In the future some people will draw so much of the higher quality of thought to them, that by it they will accomplish what some would call miracles...

> Before men knew how to use electricity there was as much of it as today, and with the same power as today; but so far as our convenience was concerned it was quite useless as a message-bearer, because there was lack of knowledge to direct it...

> The tremendous power of human thought is with us all today very much in a similar condition. It is wasted, because we do not know how to concentrate and direct it...

> Whatever the mind is set upon, or whatever it keeps most in view, that it is bringing to it, and the continual thought or imagining must at least take form and shape in the world of seen and tangible things...

> ...this fact is the cornerstone of your happiness or misery, permanent health and prosperity, or poverty. It needs to be kept as much as possible in mind...

THE ANSWER: THOUGHTS ARE THINGS

> Our thought is the unseen magnet, ever attracting its correspondence in things seen and tangible. As we realize this more and more clearly, we shall become more and more careful to keep our minds set in the right direction. We shall be more and more careful to think happiness and success instead of misery and failure…
>
> When we realize that we can and do think ourselves into what we are, as regards health, wealth and position, we realize also that we have found in ourselves "the pearl of great price," and we hasten to tell our neighbour that he may seek and find in himself this pearl and power also… through the power it gives them to add to the general wealth and happiness…

New light, new knowledge and new results in human life and all it involves, are coming to this earth.

Here is this author telling people of over a hundred years ago that this could be a time of miracles. Is this type of reading what inspired the pioneers and early business magnates such as Henry Ford to achieve success? Did they take the sharing of the "pearl of great price" to heart? Today, in this current century, if you came to realize your personal power; who would you share this knowledge with?

_____

_____

_____

Chapter Nine- THE GOD IN YOURSELF

In Chapter 9, Mulford connects our growing knowledge of our power with the fact that power comes from the Power of God. He likens it again to electricity. Electricity has been on earth since its inception. It has only been harnessed by man in the last few centuries.

Just like electricity, the power of our brain has been with mankind for tens of thousands of years. Throughout those years, some of mankind has come to realize that there is a Power to thinking. Some have learned how to use it or to partially use it. What is exciting about this is that today we are learning ever more how to harness this power and focus this energy through the power within our own thoughts and our own brains.

> Love is an element which though physically unseen is as real as air or water. It is an acting, living, moving force, and in that far greater world of life all around us, of which physical sense is unaware, it moves in waves and currents like those of the ocean.

> The Christ of Nazareth once bade certain of his followers not to worship him. "Call me not good" said he. "There is none good save God alone." Christ said, "I am the way and life," meaning, as the text interprets itself to me, that as to certain general laws of which he was aware, and by which he also as a spirit was governed, he knew and could give certain information. But he never did assert that his individual life, with all the human infirmity or defect that he had "taken upon him," was to be strictly copied.

> He did pray to the Infinite Spirit of Good for more strength, and deliverance from the sin of fear when his spirit quailed at the prospect of his crucifixion; and in so doing, he conceded that he, as a spirit (powerful as he was) needed help as much as any other spirit; and knowing this, he refused to pose himself before his followers as God, or the Infinite, but told them that when they desired to bow before that

almighty and never to be comprehended power, out of which comes every good at the prayer or demand of human mind, to worship God alone,--God, the eternal and unfathomable moving power of boundless universe; the power that no man has ever seen or ever will see.

That Power is today; working on, and in, and through, every man, woman, and child on this planet. Or, to use the biblical expression, it is, "God working in us and through us." We are all parts of the Infinite Power-- a power ever carrying us up to higher, finer, happier grades of being.

God is working in and through us.

Chapter Ten - THE HEALING AND RENEWING FORCE OF SPRING

Mulford speaks of the importance of rest.

> In the kingdom of nature, we find periods of rest constantly alternating with periods of activity.

> When man recognizes the fact that he cannot use his body year after year... and when he does recognize the fact that through placing himself oftener in restful and receptive states, as do tree, bird, and animal in their natural state, he will then, through receiving far more of this element, enjoy a far greater health of body, elasticity of muscle, vigour and brilliancy of mind. He would also have other senses and powers awakened within him, whose existence is still doubted by most people.

> The thought-power which works most while the body is relatively inactive is really the strongest and ultimately prevails. It is subtle, noiseless, unseen.

Gleaned from Chapter 10 was the importance of rest, of good sleep to regenerate the mind. Give us our daily bread, but also give us our daily rest. Our current society has lost that day of rest that used to be mandated by church and state. Stores are open seven days a week, some twenty four hours a day. When can we rest?

Mindful meditation is growing in popularity in recent years and is supported by many medical practitioners. Individuals are trying to create their own time of rest, maybe not a whole day, but at least a period of time to rest. This regeneration gives the brain time to attract to you what you have consciously asked for and believed in. It is meant for mankind to do. Rest, relax, rejuvenate, and receive!

Chapter Eleven - IMMORTALITY IN THE FLESH

Mulford feels that belief is a key.

> "Thy faith hath made thee whole" said the Christ of Judea to a man who was healed. To us this passage interprets itself as meaning that the person healed had an innate power of believing that he could be healed. This power was of his own spirit (and not of Christ's) so acted on his body instantly to cure his infirmities. Christ was a means of awakening this power in that man's spirit. But Christ himself did not give the person that power. It was latent in the person healed. Christ woke it into life.

> ...the eternal fact is that all things in this planet are ever moving forward to greater refinement; greater powers; and greater possibilities.

Health and Healing are inspirational. I just connected with someone I knew from the child-raising time of our lives. Our sons had gone through school together. In recent years, the mom had fought against disease and thankfully is in healthy remission. Was it her healthy belief that helped heal her? Each day she now thinks, *If this was my last day today, did I live it doing what I wanted to do?* This message can speak to each of us. She is a strong vibrant woman with lots to live for. Think health! Think vitality! Live life fully!

Have you heard of or experienced a health miracle? What do you think helped the healing?

_____

_____

_____

In Appendix V to this book are re-printed excerpts from *Thoughts Are Things* with added notations to explain "why" Prentice Mulford's methodology just might work. Direct quotes from *Thoughts Are Things* are in italics.

Historical seekers and writers Mulford and Fillmore (and modern-day writer Travis Taylor) all suggest that there are other possibilities, other realities out there waiting for us to choose from.

A tool might be to focus on the reality that you want for yourself. And when someone or something perturbs you, say, "You are not in my reality," or "That is not my reality; my reality is _____". Ha!

You can also declare, to no one in particular, "Thank goodness you are not going to be in my afterlife with me." Or you could say, "I am going to Heaven and obviously you are not." Try to immediately pivot to what you do want in your current reality.

Pivot

Pivoting is a tool that the seeker Elizabeth Hay speaks of in her inspirational teachings, especially when dealing with negativity and negative people. She went through a major medical crisis that she pivoted away from herself by saying and reiterating that she was healthy and whole and well-structured. Her health was regained.

Encourage all to pivot their thoughts. If you or they don't want something to happen, challenge it or them by asking "What *do* you want?"

For example:

> It's another rainy day. What do I want? I want a sunny day, so pivot! Think about a sunny day. Think, *Look at this wonderful sunshine!*
>
> This boss is driving me nuts! Pivot! It is so great now that my boss is listening to my suggestions.

Negative people are so draining on our personal energy. To counter this, keep gently asking them, "Well, what do you want to have happen?" because obviously they aren't happy with what they perceive is happening. Questioning them pivots their negative thinking.

Do you see how it can work? Pivot! Your world will change and be lighter! Positivity trumps negativity every time.

THE ANSWER: THOUGHTS ARE THINGS

Who is the negative person in your life? How could you Pivot them to think more positively?

_____

_____

_____

Suggest

Knowledge-seeker Joseph Murphy Ph.D. wrote a number of books; one of the most inspiring is *The Power of Your Subconscious Mind*. The book talks of people being magnetized through the miracle working power in your subconscious mind to be full of confidence and faith.

Murphy writes of infinite wisdom, infinite power, and infinite supply being all that is necessary. Knowledge of all kinds comes from the infinite intelligence in your subconscious. Prayers are answered by the law of your mind—that being the law of belief. Your mind's belief is the thought of your mind. The "thought of your mind" on your subconscious brings to you all your life's experiences and events. Murphy felt that the universal law of action and reaction is how prayers are answered.

Thought is the action; reaction is the response from the subconscious mind.

It is best to fill your mind with positive things, such as peace, health, goodwill, and harmony to attract to your life wonderful things. Control your thoughts; control your mind.

He is yet another author that spoke of the world within creating the world without, just as the writings on the ancient emerald tablet express. Vital forces flow from the subconscious energies as instructed by your conscious thoughts that you believe and accept to be true.

> All that is true, all that is noble, all that is just and pure, all that is lovable and gracious, whatever is excellent and admirable—fill your thoughts with these things.
> —Philippians 4:8

Release the powers of your subconscious mind. Great people, men and women of all ages, had this ability, this secret of being in contact with the power within. You can also be in touch with this power.

Believe that you have this power to connect to deep within to heal, to prosper yourself and to inspire others. The depth of your belief must be strong.

But how do we do this? The powerful force of suggestion comes into play. I "suggest" that I have all the time in the world to do what I want to do. I "suggest" that money is no concern, that I have the finances to travel anywhere in the world, funds to help family and friends. Do not think, *Oh, woe is me! Only the rich can afford to travel.* Instead, think *I am rich; I have the resources to travel anywhere I want, to help anyone I want, to donate to whatever group in need I want.* By writing this down I have made a statement of my suggestions and they have come to be. My changed thoughts have caused the conditions of my life, my destiny to change.

Make wise choices, and make a definite plan on how to connect and stay connected with your subconscious mind.

What do you want to suggest right now to your subconscious? This is where you get to become the great pretender. What do you want to pretend? The written word is powerful. Write it down.

_____

_____

_____

THE ANSWER: THOUGHTS ARE THINGS

Concentration

Seekers such as Charles and Cora Fillmore wrote the book *Teach us to Pray* in support of their Unity ministry, with the first printing in 1941. Their book talks of the omnipresence, omniscience and omnipotence of being—yes, just being here and existing on earth.

Here is someone else who also advocated that the kingdom of God is within you. This was the first book in all my reading that spoke of the power of an unknown word that was lost to mankind and was impossible to pronounce.

Searching for this word initiated my search for the origin of the word "God". The Fillmores felt that the lost word might be veiled in the word *Yahveh* and wrote about the *Word* being *Logos*. The Greek term *logos* has no equivalent in the English language.

To pray, they advocated "the concentration in silence" and "concentration on an imaginary point", basically closing your ears and your eyes so that you turn your attention inward. They believed that concentrated prayer is how to make contact with the "Super mind" that Jesus referred to as "the Father". They write of Jesus bringing the universal energy of life to all so that life could be lived more abundantly.

There is also an interesting section on "Light". I am the light of the world; you are the light of the world. This inner light is the light and intelligence to all creation. The book quotes the Apostle James, who wrote, "Every good gift and every perfect gift is from above, coming from the Father of lights."

The Gospel of John also says, "In him was Life and the life was the light of men. The light shineth in the darkness and the darkness apprehended it not... there was the true light, even the light which lighteth every man, coming into the world. I came that ye might have life and have it abundantly." Cora and Charles interpreted Light and Life to be connected as the Intelligence of God in action. "Knowing" is "Life".

The Fillmores also mention the following quote from Genesis 3:22: "Behold, the man is become as one of us." Again, who is this "us"? It is a clear statement that has survived the translations of ancient myths and the passage of time. Are the "us" beings the Creator of the first spark of Life? The Creator of the first spark of Light? The Cause of the first Energy?

Could you find that spark? Would it energize you to think that you are full of Light and Life? Circle one:

        Yes   No   Maybe

Watchers
Ancient Sumerians stone tablets texts describe other worldly beings (the Anunnaki) coming to earth to mine gold to save their lives and their planet. To do so, they created humans to do the work. Is this where the biblical reference to "Watchers" comes from?

Was the earth flooded by one of the "Anunnaki gods" to eliminate the earthlings and the watchers who had procreated with the humans? Was mankind saved by yet another Anunnaki god who felt there were some redeeming values in these humans and therefore forewarned Noah of the flood? There are lots of things to speculate on and to think about, aren't there? We may have started out to be worker bees, but here we are made in the image, and potentially with the knowledge and power of our creator(s).

Visualization and Auto-Suggestion
Napoleon Hill was a seeker who advocated that if we learn to think like wealthy people, we can discover wealth and success.

THE ANSWER: THOUGHTS ARE THINGS

His book *Think and Grow Rich* gives examples of the millionaires and intelligent people of the early 1900s and how they achieved success through having a strong desire for that success.

These people visualized and believed in that success and used tools such as auto-suggestion, vivid focussed imagination, organized planning, and persistence. The driving force of success was their own ability to harness the power of their own thoughts and then connect those thoughts to the subconscious mind.

Here again was a book that said "thoughts are things"—and are such powerful things that, when combined with persistence, purpose and "burning desire", could translate into real objects and real wealth. As mentioned before, it was Napoleon Hill who suggested we create a group of imaginary counsellors to emulate and seek advice from. Perhaps by emulating we can become more like the inspirational people in our group.

The Team

Here is an example of how I visualize my team:

Leonardo da Vinci sits in a room, doodling drawings and calculations on a scroll. His hair, beard and robes flow about him in an elegant array.

Rhonda Byrne, the Australian writer, is also present, animatedly discussing her new book idea with Leon Uris; both are seated in carved oak chairs cushioned with royal blue velvet.

Leon has written his share of best-sellers "in his day" and is giving pointers on plots that could be readily adapted to the big screen.

Rhonda is well-dressed, pointing to her financial success in promoting her book *The Secret*.

Leon's attire is casual, with his hair receding and a bit long, touching his open collared-shirt.

They are seated at a circular table, as an even-sized circle gives each participant equal standing. As Chair, I did not want to elevate nor diminish my standing with the counsellors, so a round light oak table with a central ornately-carved pedestal works fine.

To my left is a large deeply-curved shield carved out of the same light oak, extending floor to ceiling, touching the table but with the opening facing away. By the radiating glow, I knew it was occupied.

The remaining six oak carved chairs are empty, ready for their occupants.

This is the start of my personal group of counsellors.

There is no such thing as something for nothing. The Andrew Carnegie secret is that *an idea* is the beginning for all earned riches, all achievement. So be success-conscious. Clearly write down the desired goals, with steps to achievement. Use self-suggestion to build character. Here is mine:

> "I desire to be a successful, wealthy, widely acclaimed writer sought after for talk shows and inspirational speaking tours." "The steps are to complete the writing, publish and market it well."

Write down at least one goal for yourself and three steps to achieve that goal.

_____
_____
_____

THE ANSWER: THOUGHTS ARE THINGS

1. _____
   _____

2. _____
   _____

3. _____
   _____

Hill's own group were powerful inspirational people from the past and from the present, and in imaginary council meetings he stated exactly what he wanted to learn, to acquire from each of them. The more he imagined or dreamed these meetings, the more real the imaginary figures became.

In one of the imaginary sessions, Thomas Edison told Hill that he was destined to witness the discovery of the secret of life and that in time Hill would observe that life consists of great swarms of energy or intelligent eternal entities. Hill's own thoughts and desires would be the magnets that would attract these units of life.

Edison was still alive at the time, and when Hill spoke to Edison about this imaginary conversation, Edison apparently told him that the dream was more a reality than he may have imagined it to be. Hill was very concerned that he himself was losing touch with reality and stopped attempting to imagine counsellors for some time. He later returned to the practice.

Reading this book gave me the idea of creating my own group of imaginary counsellors. I had started with Leonardo Da Vinci, being an admirer of his vast futuristic intelligence and amazing art. But mainly Leonardo was there because of a dream. It was one of those nights where I slept really deeply. Somewhere in the murky dream world I saw the form of a man in robes. He turned and looked at me, right into my eyes, and then turned back and walked away. I rarely remember dreams, but the image of an ancient face with wise eyes, as well as his long hair and beard remained with me. The intensity with which he had looked at me was disconcerting; it felt like he was an ancient soul looking into my soul. It wasn't until I was once more at the bookstore that I saw the exact same face on the cover of a book; I realized it was Leonardo Da Vinci that had looked at me in my dream. So I bought the book, *How to Think like Leonardo da Vinci* by Michael J. Gelb.

My next step was to add two more writers to my group of imaginary counsellors: Leon Uris and Rhonda Bryne, who I felt I could ask advice of for this book project. Then I added Warren Buffet to sit in one of those cushioned oak chairs as someone whose down-to-earth common sense (combined with wealth) I would be happy to emulate.

I also included my own mother in a place at the conference table. She was a hard-working woman, admired for her strength and tenacity in raising a family on her own through hard times. During periods of stress, I visualize speaking with her at the farm kitchen table while she has her favourite cup full of instant coffee. Sometimes at bedtime I imagine being close to her and it takes me back to a more innocent time of my life. I fall asleep despite the stress, wake up refreshed, and take on the new day.

I still continue to add counsellors, such as members of my immediate and extended family, to draw strength from or to just to be my "happy thought."

Once a week, take time to still your mind; state the purpose of the meeting and call your counsellors to the table. Visualize each one as they sit down. Ask the question, whatever it may be, such as, "I need your help with_____." "What are your thoughts on _____?" Then imagine each one speaking to you. The effect is pretty powerful.

THE ANSWER: THOUGHTS ARE THINGS

Could you create a support group of imaginary counsellors? Name two people you would want in your group.

1. _____
   _____

2. _____
   _____

In Napoleon Hill's book it also was stated that thoughts mixed with emotions constitute a magnetic force to connect with other similar related thoughts. Other riveting statements from the book are "secret of life", "life consists of swarms of energy or intelligent eternal entities" and "thoughts and desires are magnets to attract these units of life". Light orbs, magnetic thinking...

This theme repeats again and again with many authors. So what did all these great New Age writers and New Thought leaders have in common? They all have an intuitive belief in the all-saving power of healthy mind attitudes, and in the conquering efficacy of courage, hope and trust. They believed in healing through prayer, of being one with His creation. They all appeared to believe in God, and in the existence of Jesus.

Attributing divine powers to people is also known as Apotheosis, existing since ancient history. These concepts are not New Thought but are ancient Biblical wisdom, particularly illustrated in the New Testament and the parables in the Lost Gospels of the first centuries AD. The pathway to enlightenment, to the Answer; continues.

Seekers in Modern Times

Modern-day Seekers have come to the forefront seeking the "why" and the "how" of what previous seekers were alluding to as being possible. These are also seekers of the wisdom of "Sophia", *gnosis*, of knowledge. The researchers and scientists strive to find the facts behind the miracle. Technology is advancing so quickly, doubling; tripling what is available to study and what might benefit mankind. In many cases the capability is now here to review, test and explain ancient cures, ancient theories.

Knowledge Seekers
The next group of seekers was quite surprising. They not only fit in as ancient seekers but as modern-day seekers of gnosis, of knowledge. These are the societies of Freemasons. The origins of the name and of the group go way back to pre-biblical Egyptian times. Masons were the workers of stone, the builders of the temples. To enable them to work across different areas of the country, societies of master builders were formed; therefore they were "free" masons.

Woven in here is the legend of Hiram Abiff. The Bible states that Hiram was skilled to work with many things:

> …skilful to work in gold, and in silver, in brass, in iron, in stone, and in timber, in purple, in blue, and in fine linen, and in crimson: also to grave any manner of graving and to find out every device which shall be put to him…
> — (2 Chronicles 4:14)

He was a master craftsman, associated with King Huram of Tyre, and was sent to help build the temple that Solomon wanted to build

> …to the name of the Lord my God.
> — (2 Chronicles 2:4)

The temple was to house

> ...the ark of the covenant of the Lord out of the city of David which is Zion.
> — (2 Chronicles 5:2)

> There was nothing in the ark save the two tablets which Moses put therein.
> — (2 Chronicles 5:10)

There was a secret word shared between Hiram Abiff and two others, now lost, and sought after to this day. Or has the word been found?

There are massive amounts of research to read on the entire history of the society. Things of interest were the quotations from the lost gospel of Thomas that the Mason research highlighted.

Scripture 1: And he said, *"**Whoever discovers the interpretation of these sayings will not taste death.**"*

Scripture 2: Jesus said, *"**Those who seek should not stop seeking until they find. When they find, they will be disturbed. When they are disturbed, they will marvel, and will reign over all. [And after they have reigned they will rest.]**"*

Scripture 5: Jesus said, *"**Know what is in front of your face, and what is hidden from you will be disclosed to you. For there is nothing hidden that will not be revealed. [And there is nothing buried that will not be raised.]**"*

And Matthew 13:35 says, "I will utter things which have been kept secret from the foundation of the world."

The reading also emphasized that throughout time, the Word had not changed; the real Word and the Way to the Light had not changed. For all who seek it, God's Light rays are available to them.

There they were again—people talking about The Word, The Way and The Light. There definitely is something to this pathway for mankind to take note of.

Have you thought about Word, Way and Light? What do those three words mean to you?

The Word_____

The Way_____

The Light_____

Healing

Why and how can there be miracle healing? Healing of biblical times, healing of modern times. Doctors continue to be amazed at the unexpected recovery of "terminal" patients. Is the power of their mind a factor? Do they somehow cure from within? Do the patients who focus their thoughts on being cured do better than those who give up? That can now be studied, tested and documented to develop better healing methods.

There is the healing practice of hand acupressure. This is where the healer's middle two fingers on both hands are pressed onto two parts of the subject's body to promote healing.

Tests are proving that there really are human energy fields, some so strong that they are indeed capable of healing. Yes, healing energy from the electrical impulses of human cells and magnetic fields around human organs are now measurable. Dr. John Zimmerman has studied therapeutic touch and has measured the bio-magnetic field emanating from the hands of healing practitioners.

There is something to this, but the patient must believe it to be true for the healing to really take hold. Did the healer that was

THE ANSWER: THOUGHTS ARE THINGS

Jesus have a strong human energy field? Is that how some miracles were performed by him? The only place that he was not able to perform miracles was in his home town where no one believed he was the Messiah. He was just Joe's son—you know, the carpenter.

Is belief a factor in being healed? Why do you think it helps? Write down your thoughts.

_____

_____

_____

Reality Dimensions

Are multiple realities truly a possibility? Some people experience feelings of déjà vu, the feeling they have been somewhere before or have done something before the present experience. What would cause these feelings?

Physicist Max Planck, a quantum theory founder, said, "All matter originates and exists only by virtue of a force which brings the particles of an atom to vibration which holds the atom together. We must assume behind this force is the existence of a conscious and intelligent mind. This mind is the matrix of all matter."

You might have to read that one through a few times: *The conscious and intelligent mind is the matrix, the "glue" of all matter.*

Quantum theory says that thought or consciousness is the building block of the universe. Quantum physicists of the past and present are trying to prove or disprove that the possibility of multiple realities, multiple universes exists.

Light is a wave until it is observed, and when observed it becomes a particle. If your consciousness expects something to be there, it will be there. Now, doesn't that just blow you away? Your reality, the substance of your universe, may only be the accumulation of your thought and consciousness. Change your thoughts, and create, or change, your reality.

It was the scientific research into light particles (and particularly atomic particles) that revealed that an atomic particle does not appear to have a single exact location. Instead, the particles have the ability to exist in more than one place at the same time. Is the answer true—that these particles exist in parallel universes, and not only in our universe? The work of leading scientists and physicists suggest the existence of such multiple universes.

Time travel has been the stuff of movies and box office hits. Reality dimensions, quantum jumping; now the scientific community says – maybe this could be accomplished. Entrepreneur Burt Goldman advocates a program of quantum jumping that revolves partially around meditation and twin visualization. Whether you believe that this is really quantum jumping into another reality or not, it does provide a great method for meditation.

Most would never think of visualizing themselves as a twin who had made different choices and therefore was living in a different reality. It is very hard to feel and imagine a different life, a different world. It is harder still to try to see yourself there. Unless you are really focused on yourself, you probably don't dwell on what others see when they look at you.

Most people are not prone to gazing that much in a mirror. Yet to imprint what you look like enough to project that image into your vision board or dream life, you would have to do a lot more gazing than you usually would, such as while brushing your teeth, shaving, or doing your hair.

A visioning tool might be to do something exactly like that. Take a mirror with you to your quiet spot for a fifteen-minute stare-down each day; put a big smile on your face and then close your eyes, bringing two fingers of one or both hands to the spot between your eyebrows.

Project that image of you into how you want your day to go, into where you would like to holiday, into the house where you want to live, and how happy and peaceful you would like to feel. If you can imprint this image of *you*, where you want *you* to be, that is the strongest vision board that there can be.

Close your eyes. Can you "see" you? Circle one:

                Yes   No   Maybe

It is not easy, is it?

All this visioning and all this knowledge of how to keep the energy vibrating can feel like too much to think about at times—wouldn't you agree? Here is another tool to use throughout your day:

Angel Numbers

There are followers of numerology that study number patterns in the Bible giving emphasis to such numbers as the number three being a symbol of completeness, The Triune God and the divine manifestation and divine perfection of things physical, moral and spiritual. The number three and the number seven are the most commonly used in the Bible. The seventh being a day of rest, Enoch being the seventh from Adam and the ultimate forgiveness measurement is seventy times seven.

Some cultures feel there is significance to numerical sequences that can provide guidance in your life. I have found that noting numbers can be mood lifting. Find a book on angel numbers; there are a number of authors to try, some probably better than others. I purchased a book written by Doreen Virtue. There is a basic pattern in the books to keep in mind:

Derivatives of:

> Zero, 0: This number is to be interpreted that Divine guidance of God or other ascended masters is right at hand to reassure you, to talk to you.
>
> One, 1: Keep focussed on your positive desires as your thoughts are instantly manifesting.
>
> Two, 2: A message of "keep the faith", steady as you go; things are working out as they should. Keep believing in positive outcomes.
>
> Three, 3: Feel that you have a strong connection with God or with your chosen protecting ascended master, whether that is Jesus, Buddha or more. Feel loved, feel guided.
>
> Four, 4: You are to think of angels being with you, around you. Ask for their help, and feel secure and supported by heavenly beings.
>
> Five, 5: Change is coming, which is always positive, but ask for help to manage the change. Out with the old, in with the new; keep your happy thought strong to keep the change positive.
>
> Six, 6: This is a nudge that your thoughts are heavy with stress and fear, and that the material mind is too full of worry. The materialistic mind is suppressing the spiritual mind. Ask for help to strengthen your spiritual mind and bring it back to the forefront.
>
> Seven, 7: Lucky seven—keep up the great work! You are on the illuminated path. You are supported, and doors of opportunity are opening.
>
> Eight, 8: This is a favourable sign of abundance, of prosperity; it is auspicious and indicates financial

support for you. Think of money flowing in your direction.

Nine, 9: This is a game-changer, a notification to get to work on your divine life purpose. You've completed the prerequisites, so now it's time to get ready for action steps. Ask your spiritual mind for what you need to get motivated or to clarify what to do.

The angel number books give an explanation for each number sequence between 10 and 999 which are variations on the base number between 0 and 9 as indicated above. Sequences can be energy and positive mood boosters. For example sequence (123) can mean simplify your life; numbers (234) may mean that you have powerful allies in the angels around you; the sequence (987) says keep up the good work, you are on the right path with your finances, your career, and your spiritual life.

We are surrounded by numbers—on the digital clock, in our workplace, on licence plates, and street signs on our daily commutes to work. It's probably not worth getting terribly excited about seeing a single-digit number. But perhaps if you were to see triple digits or often see double-digit numbers you might consider using the glimpses of these numbers to keep your spirits up. Happy thoughts around abundance can be associated with (888), seeing (444) may generate the feeling of being loved, noting (222) should foster a belief in positive outcomes, and seeing (777) can make you smile thinking "what if I won the big one".

Numbers can be a booster shot throughout the day at any moment. Keep that spiritual, emotional, magnetic energy field up and stimulate your conscious mind. Send good messages to your subconscious level. If you come across an interesting double or triple number sequence in your day, smile and put an "ask" or a happy thought out there.

What number sequences do you want to see? Write them down.

_____

_____

_____

The Next Life

One of the last books that I was "led" to read was about a near-death experience that happened to a neurosurgeon, Eben Alexander M.D. He was not seeking this experience of bacterial meningitis that badly damaged the neocortex of his brain. The six-day coma shut down the auditory and visual part of his brain along with the rest of his body.

As the coma became prolonged, there was a ninety-seven percent chance of mortality, and yet on the seventh day he opened his eyes. He was alert, and once the breathing tube was removed, he said, "Thank you." He also said, "All is well… Don't worry…all is well."

He later wrote the book *Proof of Heaven* to describe what he experienced and "saw" in the six days that he was in complete brain and body shut-down in the coma. He talks of first being in a state of pulsating, pounding, primordial darkness. Then he was approached by something spinning which then visually became radiating filaments of light that broke up the darkness, along with a beautiful living sound. The centre of the light opened up and he was drawn through to a new world. In his words, he said it was "brilliant, vibrant, ecstatic, and stunning."

You have to read the book to get the full scope of what he saw, who helped him to understand what he was seeing, and how he felt. I was drawn to his description of flocks of shimmering, scintillating, transparent orb-like angel beings surging across the skies with joyful perfect song.

He also wrote of experiencing a feeling that he was near a being that was the "source", the Creator of all that he was seeing. The sound that he remembered hearing was "Om" as he felt the love of this presence. Without language, he absorbed knowledge of multiple universes, advanced intelligence, higher dimensions, of worlds of overarching divine reality from which at any time or place are accessible in our world.

The whole experience was life-changing for him, and the message this man received and now passes on to us all is that you are loved, and that unconditional love is the basis of all the realities and is at the base of all that exists.

Talk about giving reassurance of a life after our walk on this earthly planet! Again, the emphasis was on Light, on Knowledge, on Realities, on Love. These words, these emotions keep showing up time and time again in the readings.

Do you feel loved? Do you love someone? Write their name down.

_____
_____
_____

What if a voice came from the sky or from inside your head and said YOU ARE LOVED? What emotion would you feel?

_____
_____
_____

14.
SEEKING THE POWER OF THE BRAIN

What the authors and inspirational leaders of a century ago could not quite prove is the mechanics of how the thought process worked. They knew that focused thought and focused prayer brought great things into existence. Research had not yet shown that the human brain had the vibration capability within it to use the Power of what they spoke and wrote about.

Your brain has an almost-perfect memory. One proof of this is that people under hypnosis can remember every thought or word and visualize every step, every look. So what is hypnosis that it can do this? Hypnosis provides a state of "alert relaxation".

How can we give our brains the right stimulation to achieve this alert relaxation so that our perfect memory and our powerful brain can do its best thinking for us? Meditation is a good step. Breathing slowly is an excellent way to slow down your body and life so that the focus can be on your brain. With the first few deep breaths, think of drawing in nothing; just feel the air come in through your nostrils, filling your chest cavity. Then start to think that each deep breath is Life or that each breath is drawing in that empty space that contains all things and that it brings Knowledge into your chest cavity as it rises up to energize your brain. Smile.

Just try that; deep breathing and thinking as an exercise. Did that quiet your life, energize your mind, and make you feel good, if even for a minute?

Is the pineal gland in the brain a control for the energy of the body? This gland is a photo-sensitive organ connected to the eye through a nerve and is directly connected to the central nervous system. Ancient people considered the pineal gland as the seat of the soul and suggested that when mediating, to hold our attention a little above the place between our eyebrows. So is it a control or just a conduit?

Some that meditate think of that energy-directing gland and think of it connecting to the thinking "conscious" part of brain in the crown chakra, which is the part of your brain that is below the soft spot that you had as a baby. They feel that the spot between the eyebrows on a human, sometimes referred to as the *Adjna*, is a direct connection to the depth of the brain.

It was in these readings that the authors touched on auras and colours that surround our bodies. Do we have an etheric physical body emitting a light blue/grey light, an emotional body with a swirling mass of energy around us? With that etheric, emotional body, do we have a visible yellow glow around our head and shoulders showing our basic beliefs, intellect and personal power and understanding?

Have you ever been "drawn" to be close to someone? Some people seem to emit such energy or calmness or strength that you want to talk to them or be in their circle of conversation. How do they emit that? Can you try to emulate that calmness and strength?

Name someone that you enjoy being with:

Let's talk "Brain Power"

Dr. Stuart Hameroff's work researched microtubules. What are microtubules? Well, they are a major part of cell division, of cell function all over the body. The way the microtubules functioned led him to wonder if they were controlled by some sort of computing, some very complex computing and significant operations.

If we could understand the operations of microtubules in brain cells, would this then lead to an understanding of consciousness? As an anaesthetist, he studied how the anaesthetic he administered specifically affected neural microtubules. Patients lost consciousness and did not feel the effect of the surgery being performed on them.

Our bodies are made of cells; therefore we are crawling with microtubules of one form or the other as they are the key to the cell cytoskeleton structure and cell division. Microtubules maintain your cell structure; they provide the transport of intercellular substances.

Visualize microtubules as being long hollow cylinders that are made up of tubular polymers of tubulin. Next, envision the tubulin being long parallel strings of proto filaments forming the building block of the microtubule structure. These tubulin dimmers are formed by globular proteins that are made up of a positive and negative charge—alpha and beta.

This gives the microtubules polarity, a positive charge at one end of the hollow tube, and negative at the other. The tubes can grow or retract as needed. There appears to be some spin cycle that happens due to the opposite electrical charge on each end. Now, visualize that each microtubule is very, very small (only up to twenty-five micrometres long). Conceptualize this as being an extremely tiny and invisible dot on an extremely pointy end of a dressmaker's pin. Proteins bind to the microtubules and help regulate their dynamic activity.

If scientists read this, they would probably cringe at the explanation above, but the true detailed explanation is extremely complicated and long, and is full of very complicated terms. It would take a scientist to explain it and would only be truly understood by another scientist.

The goal is to get you, the reader, thinking about the growth and flow of cells within your body, particularly your brain cells. The hollow part of the microtubule is where the flow happens. Possibly the positive and negative charge at the end is what draws the flow, the thinking along. The spin cycle within the hollow accelerates the activity. Your thinking may well be the result of electrical impulses zipping around your brain through the microtubules of your brain cells.

Close your eyes. Try to tighten the skin on the back of your head and over your skull; breathe and then relax. Think "Success", and then smile. Can you imagine your thoughts flowing through tiny tubes? Circle one:

$$\text{Yes} \quad \text{No} \quad \text{Maybe}$$

Now, just think if you could focus that activity, those electrical impulses; you might develop conscious control of your thoughts.

Consciousness...
Another brain power-seeker was Roger Penrose. He felt that the brain could complete many functions that were beyond the scope of a standard computer. This again reiterates that brains are not becoming like computers—it is computers that are becoming more like brains.

THE ANSWER: THOUGHTS ARE THINGS

He too wondered about a consciousness connection. Consciousness is the awareness of something around you or of something within you. Quantum theory principles seem to provide a non-algorithmic process through which consciousness might arise. Objective Reduction (OR) or quantum wave reduction could link the brain to space-time geometry.

Together, Hameroff and Penrose explored the possibility that microtubules performed a quantum function in the brain and formulated a model of consciousness called Orch-OR, orchestrated objective reduction. The quantum function meaning that the smallest unit of change happens in neuron microtubules to produce consciousness. The brain network may process information faster than any other network.

Again, the idea arises that possibly our own brain "computer" can examine all possibilities at once, and therefore arrive at the best choice, the best answer for you to proceed with again and again and again.

Controlling your Consciousness...

The book *Mind and the Brain* by J. Schwartz M.D. and Sharon Begley confirmed to me that we do have the power to enact change on our brains using focussed thinking for the betterment of our lives. It is an amazing summary of research on brain development, explaining not only what your brain can do, but where in your brain thought "traffic" happens. Have you thought about your brain lately—what it looks like and what it does? It is more than just grey matter; there are some pretty high-functioning things going on in there.

There is not one part of the brain that is more important than the other. All are needed for a fully functioning human. A scan of your brain from the top shows an oval shape with roughly two halves and four lobes.

Cerebrum: Divided into two sides, left and right, this constitutes two-thirds of your brain mass. The two halves are separated by a deep groove and connected by neuron branches named *corpus callosum*. Think of the cerebrum as the glue that connects each of its four specialized lobes and other brain structures, because it is positioned over and around most of them.

Visualize next the cerebrum as having an outer layer called the cerebral cortex, whose neurons are packed together and control most of your body functions, motor skills, the senses, language, reasoning and that elusive state of consciousness.

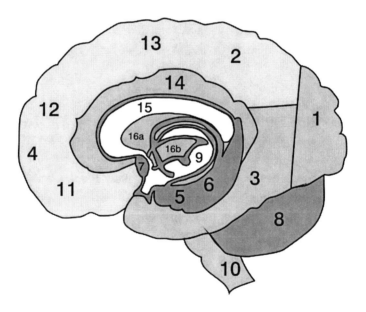

The four lobes of the cerebrum each have specific functioning:

THE ANSWER: THOUGHTS ARE THINGS

1. The Occipital Lobe, Occipital Cortex (vision) is your vision connector, processing the visual data that is routed elsewhere to be identified and stored.

2. The Parietal Lobe (movement) is your sensory gatherer, receiving body sensory information, also calculating where objects are located and the speed that they are travelling at.

3. Your Temporal Lobe (language) has your emotions, hearing and memory data storage banks with language being on the left side.

4. The Frontal Lobe (planning) is like a command centre, the dorsolateral prefrontal circuit being our organiser and first responder to plan solutions to problems, adapt strategies, guide behaviour and manage emotional impulses in socially appropriate way. The Frontal lobe does not fully develop until young adulthood, so this may explain why as a youth we may have made some inappropriate decisions, like putting vinegar in a glass of water intended for a visiting aunt. (Good thing she had a sense of humour—my Mom didn't!)

5. Amygdala (basic emotions): This is your emotional tracker. It is constantly alert to basic survival needs and emotional reactions such as anger or fear. Only the size of an almond, it is a powerful operative deep in the limbic brain system, associated with a range of mental conditions.

6. Hippocampus (memory): Also located deep within the brain, the hippocampus processes your new memories for long-term storage. Without it, you couldn't live in the present; you'd be working only in the past with old previously-recorded memories.

7. Hypothalamus (monitor): This is your body's hall monitor for bodily functions such as body temperature, blood pressure, and appetite/weight control. Yes, this is who you can blame for your fluctuating weight problems. "It is not me—it is my hypothalamus!" At the base of the brain, where signals from the body's hormonal system and the brain interact, is where the hypothalamus resides.

8. Cerebellum (coordinate movement): Situated at the top of the brain stem, this is your control for skilled co-ordinated movement helping also with learning pathways.

9. Thalamus (action gatekeeper): Also at the top of the brain stem, the thalamus is your relay station. It processes, sorts, and directs signals from mid-brain structures and spinal cord up to the cerebrum and also back down the spinal cord to the nervous system.

10. Brain Stem (basic body functions): This is your brain connector to the spinal cord. The brain stem is the most primitive part of the human brain. It controls functions basic to the survival of humans and all animals, being heart rate, breathing, digesting foods, and sleeping.

Describing the brain sets the stage to help better to understand its importance in our seeking of knowledge. Is that more than you really wanted to know about the grey matter that you carry with you all your life?

Circle one:

                Yes   No   Maybe

Neuroplasticity refers to the capability to change our brains, create new circuit patterns and grow new brain cells. Stroke patients can sometimes restore the use of affected arms by constraining the movement of the unaffected arm and encouraging themselves to "rethink" the connection with the affected arm. Recently, the television news showed patients having electrical circuitry placed within affected limbs and then the patients stimulated the limbs using thought impulses, brain impulses to move the limbs properly once more. Now that shows the power of thinking!

Schwartz has been hugely successful in the treatment of people suffering with Obsessive Compulsive Disorder (OCD). Those with OCD have overwhelming urges to check and recheck that doors are securely locked or feel that they have to wash and rewash their hands or any number of deep and worrisome compulsions.

Schwartz has been able to identify that the brain of an OCD patient had different "mapping" than a person without OCD. His work is well documented with brain scans of OCD brains before and after his treatment method.

His method was not that of behavioural therapy where patients would be forced to face their compulsion over and over. If the fear was that of touching a dirty door knob, for example, the behavioural treatment would be to have to touch all the door knobs in a large building and not be allowed to wash their hands. This treatment was very stressful and dehumanizing for the patient. Schwartz felt there had to be another way.

He was intrigued by the idea of "directed mental force" and the research of Henry Stapp into the foundations of quantum mechanics. There was also the concept of neuroplasticity. Could the neurons in our brains make new connections, new paths, and assume new roles? He proved that the brain could indeed be "rewired" through the transforming power of the mind. Thus his patients developed self-directed neuroplasticity, new rewiring. The key was in the frontal lobe of the brain. OCD brains had thought traffic patterns different from someone without OCD.

ASK, BELIEVE, & RECEIVE

Here are a few more parts of your brain.

11. Orbital frontal cortex (appropriate social response)
12. Cerebral prefrontal cortex (logical and executive decisions)
13. Motor cortex (sensory)
14. Anterior cingulate gyrus (motivation)
15. Corpus callosum (connecting neuron branches)
16. Striatum-(receiver for neural inputs) - combination of the Caudate nucleus and Putaman

    16 a) Caudate nucleus (emotions/thoughts center) - redirects thoughts and emotions

    16 b) Putamen – redirects motor activity

Other "brain" words are TANS (Tonically Active Neurons), matrisomes and striosomes and basal ganglia outputs.

To put some of this brain functioning into a basic description, it looks like the emotion-processing amygdala (5) talks to the emotions/thought center caudate nucleus (16) through the striosomes.

>Amygala >> Striosomes >> Caudate nucleus

The thinking, reasoning cerebral prefrontal cortex (12) talks to the emotions/thought center caudate nucleus (16) through the matrisomes.

Cerebral prefrontal cortex >> Matrisomes >> Caudate nucleus

Because the TANS are between the matrisomes and the striosomes, the TANS can integrate emotion and thought and redirect the decision to the Thalamus to proceed with the activity.

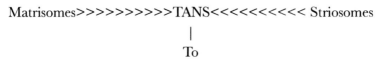

The term *Striatum* is a term for the combination of the caudate nucleus and putamen. This striatum is like the brain's receiver for neural inputs. Its components act as traffic conductors: the caudate nucleus redirects thoughts and emotions, and the putamen redirects motor activity.

Brain scans of OCD patients showed hyperactivity in the emotions and thoughts centre (caudate nucleus) (16) and hyper-metabolic activity in the error detector centre (orbital frontal cortex) (11) that is wired directly to the body's physical panic centre through the motivating anterior cingulate gyrus (14).

This hyperactivity or persistent error misfire is caused by the orbital frontal cortex, the caudate nucleus and the thalamus being hard-wired together making OCD sufferers feel something is terribly wrong. Their gate to the direct pathway in the striatum is locked open, stimulating the thalamus, accentuating cortical activity. Their indirect pathway in the striatum that inhibits cortical activity is subdued.

Schwartz documented this so well; with medical evidence, he has been able to show OCD sufferers that it is not "them"; it is not their mind or the essence of themselves that is the problem. The problem is an error in how their brains are wired to receive and send information. "It's not me, it is my OCD" is a statement that represents the first of the four steps of his treatment program: Relabeling, changing how the TANS react to OCD triggers.

Identify the compulsive symptoms as they start, then reattribute them as not "my mind" but a problem with "my brain", not with my true self. Now to teach patients how to use mental force to refocus the obsessive urges onto alternate behaviours. This is the hardest part and requires significant willpower. If successful, "why" would this mental force work? You can see that if thought and emotion can be redirected, then the motor activity can be redirected.

Persistent "wise" attention can cause volition or choice. Calcium ions flow within nerves to release neurotransmitters that cause the neuron to transmit a signal to the next one in the circuit. The dedicated attention focuses out one possibility for the brain to consider out of the all the possibilities being thrown at it. Mental imagery can activate the same regions of the brain that actual perception would.

For the OCD patient, persistent attention, persistent thinking, generates the mental force needed to refocus into alternate behaviours, like going to play piano or going to the garden instead of giving in to the impulse to wash their hands.

Schwartz figured it out that the refocusing would shut down or lessen the OCD traffic in the striatum. This changes the balance of the gating so that the indirect pathway (the inhibitor) in the striatum in the brain had more activity than the direct pathway to thalamus (the stimulator). Therefore the feelings of irrational compulsion would be subdued in the orbital frontal cortex.

The work with OCD patients offered strong evidence that wilful, mindful effort, mindful thinking can alter brain function and that with self-directed brain changes, neuroplasticity is a genuine reality.

Directed mental force sounds like deep meditation, deep thinking or possibly prayer/deep asking, doesn't it?

THE ANSWER: THOUGHTS ARE THINGS

Schwartz's book also references William James's belief in the reality of will and efficacy of mental effort: "The brain is an instrument of possibilities, not certainties," he says. He stated that consciousness will, if endowed with causal efficacy, reinforce favourable possibilities and repress unfavourable or indifferent ones.

The development of quantum physics gave the physical science to James's beliefs. He also advocated that the ability to fix one's attention on a stimulus or a thought and "hold it fast before the mind" was the act that constituted "the essential achievement of the will".

Donald Hebb, a psychologist from Canada, postulated that when presynaptic and postsynaptic neurons are simultaneously active, the synapses in the brain are strengthened and that this is the basis for learning and memory. Fifty years later it was proven that cells that fire together, wire together.

In recent years, there are now high-resolution maps of the brain that show the simplicity and complexity of the wiring in our brains. The wiring resembles an orderly 3D map or grid-like appearance similar to a street map or the weave of a carpet, if the streets or carpets were three dimensional. Visualize bundles of flat ribbon cables running in three directions in your brain: front-back, up-down and left-right. The bundles crisscross at many points to form the grid.

ASK, BELIEVE, & RECEIVE

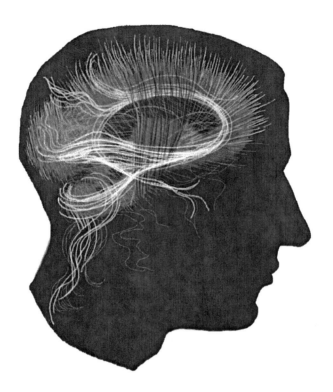

The network of nerve fibres carries impulses from one part of the brain to another. This allows different parts of the brain to communicate with each other giving the basis for all of us, including those with OCD, to rewire our brains. There is truly communicating nerve fibre cell microtubule wiring to work with.

The OCD patients in treatment were successful in rewiring, not only through the volition of free will, but through the volition of free *won't*. They "won't" let the compulsions control them any longer. Prayer and "asks" are also a form of directed free will. Maybe this is why prayers and asks with "concentration" are answered. The prayers exhibit "will" and have a network of wiring with which to work. Not all prayers or asks have equal levels of concentration and connection and therefore not all are answered.

The Dynamic Correlate of Thought
Correlate as a verb is a mutual relationship or connection in one thing that affects or depends on another. As a noun it refers to two or more related or complementary things. A correlate can be a varied interaction of processes.

The manifestation of thought in the brain is a combined physical, chemical and psychical process that happens instantly and constantly. Thought manifestation is both a verb and a noun—a dynamic correlate process.

Start by considering that every breath you take is like inhaling life energy. Now, formulate an idea. It does not have to be a light bulb moment, but something as simple as having the idea that you would like a drink of water. Your idea becomes a vibration. That vibration becomes a thought that transforms the energy required to bring that water to you, or you to the water.

Idea vibrations can become thoughts that emanate out as a transmitted force and as a magnet to attract similar vibrations of others with the same mindset. Those that you are in tune with are the ones that you may meet at the water cooler or that telephone or text you just when you think of them.

Every idea does not immediately turn into a transmitted thought. Consider that electricity can be changed into heat; the heat of electricity can be changed into light. As the light visibly radiates out, it invisibly radiates heat and invisibly has an electric current—all forms being energy transformed but never ending.

The idea vibration remains close to the source of its charge in the brain, just like electrical charge stays in the battery. Most ideas don't leave home. It is only a vibration until it is transformed into a transmission with the physiological equilibrium of persistent, concentrated psychic force, emotions, and tendencies. The idea becomes imperceptibly transformed into a thought to be sent out and shared with the universe. This is a thinking power process to strive to understand and achieve.

Conceptualize that the brain organ is like a muscle that must be exercised to maintain its good functioning and good health. Mental focus develops the natural law of use by strengthening the brain. Muscles and mental focus strengthen with use. Like a muscle, the brain will atrophy with disuse and lack of thinking.

Ignite the brain with imagination and the fire of desire. Will it to create self-development, to build inward character for the outward expression of personality. Become a positive thought-magnet. Remember that positivity annihilates negativity every time.

Desire demands expression of materialization. Imagination supplies the picture of the thing desired, and depth of desire fuels the quality of what will be received. Thinking, desiring, willing and acting out your idea is what encourages its manifestation. Ideas are powerful. Thinking is powerful. The law of attraction becomes the law of materialization by combining electrons into atoms and atoms into molecules and molecules into the form of your idea, your thinking.

For atoms there is correlation energy—Ec, defined as dynamic correlation. The non-relativistic energies of atoms, Ec can be measured using the atom's separate unlike-spin and like-spin contributions $Ec\sigma\sigma$, $Ec\alpha\beta$. The calculation results in a sum of pair energies from quantum chemistry.

Now, think of Einstein's famous formula describing energy $E = m^2$, which means energy equals mass squared. We memorized

THE ANSWER: THOUGHTS ARE THINGS

the formula in school to pass some tests. What exactly does it actually mean?

One definition describes this as a relationship of mass to energy, further stating that the universal proportionality factor between equivalent amounts of energy and mass is equal to the speed of light squared. Energy equals mass when light speed is multiplied by its own light speed. This sounds like pretty instant manifestation.

The word "quantum" comes up again and again in scientific readings to be interpreted as meaning the absolute smallest amount or a single unit. In quantum physics, a quantum is the minimum amount of physical entity involved in an interaction.

A single quantum of light is a photon. The energy of an electron bound to an atom is quantized, resulting in the stability of atoms and therefore the stability of matter in general. Quantum mechanics uses quantum as part of the fundamental framework for describing and understanding nature at the smallest length-scales.

Just when we think we have thought of the smallest quantum thing ever, scientists come up with the string theory. This depicts that the smallest particles in the universe are tiny strings of energy. These strings are a quintillion (one hundred billion billion) times smaller than a single atomic nucleus.

Not only are these strings super tiny, but they vibrate in different patterns and produce different particle properties. The conceptual framework of string theory postulates the unification of general relativity and quantum mechanics into one complete understanding of how the universe works.

One of the world's leading string theorists, Brian Greene, writes in his book *The Elegant Universe* that the universe consists of eleven dimensions. He describes the universe or space as being a fabric that tears and repairs itself constantly. This universal fabric and all matter, from the smallest quantum quarks to gargantuan supernovas, consist of and are transformed by vibrations generated by microscopically tiny loops of energy.

This could explain the "thinking substance" referred to by Wallace Wattles and other writers. Is this vibrating fabric of the universe what we are to project our vibrating thoughts into, using all that fascinating wiring in our brains? The universe's ultimate convertible currency is ENERGY.

Let's make our own formula. TE = MoM @ LS x LS

Thought Energy equals Materialization of Mass at Light Speed times Light Speed. (Could also be Mom at Light Speed, but let's keep with the thought energy line.)

Our ideas and thoughts do produce brain waves that vibrate, some of which stay within our skull, some of which transmit into the universe—and we transmit really fast! Do not stop at just thinking and desiring. Be sure to add will power, willing the vibrating idea to be.

Act as if you have received the object of your thinking and desiring. Our past thinking has produced our "today". Our present thinking will produce our "tomorrow".

We are bombarded by constant media. Unplug yourself. Turn off all the technology. Sit for a minute, and hear the quiet within. If we are exactly what we think, what do you want your brain to think about for your tomorrow? What mass do you want to materialize at the speed of light times the speed of light? Write down that vibrating idea that comes to your mind right now.

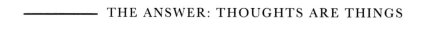

THE ANSWER: THOUGHTS ARE THINGS

Brain Exercise

There is an exercise to help focus mental images. At first glance it appears to be a group of lines or boxes. As you focus on the image, the lines become more distinct to show a three-dimensional box that can be open on the top, sides or bottom. It provides a challenge to try to visualize where the opening appears and then force your eyes and thoughts to see and hold the image of the other openings. Can you change where the box opening is?

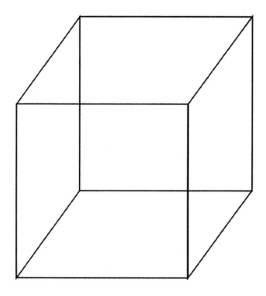

Connected consciousness

Consciousness is more than knowing and perceiving— *it is that you know that you know.*

If you recall some of the "In the Beginning" part of this book, the suggestion was that we might still have one cell of the original cells of creation. So here is some research on abiogenesis.

Divinely created billions of years ago or through a process of abiogenesis, the first cell appeared capable of reproducing and surviving. Every living organism alive today is carbon based and has that same RNA/DNA replicating capability of that first cell and every living organism is made of cells.

Living organisms all start as a single cell from its mother, with the mother's female DNA and father's male DNA; therefore the organism is not new but the same organism as their parents.

Cells continue to split in half and grow and split again and again. We are all this initial cell of creation. The first organism that ever lived on earth did not die. That DNA of the first cell is part of us.

We all have an individual consciousness that is the essence of our unique self, our mind, our soul. However, at a higher level of humanity, there might just be a "single super sub-consciousness" encompassing all of mankind and animal-kind because every organism is a shape or form from that original cell that thrived and survived.

Somewhere in each of us is a connection to each and every other person, to the single super sub-consciousness, because we all still belong to the initial originating cell. We are all cousins.

What thought "text" would you project out to all those consciousness relatives?

THE ANSWER: THOUGHTS ARE THINGS

We may really be one consciousness, but subjectively experience life in different ways. This is mankind's personal wireless internet, our universal mind. If this is true, let's use our power of single super sub-consciousness to think, to ask for world peace and harmony across all continents, across all consciousness. The greatest of these is love, and on this hangs the law of the One God common to the Abrahamic faiths and the word of the prophets.

As written in the Old Testament:

> Thou shalt not avenge, nor bear any grudge against the children of thy people, but thou shalt love thy neighbour as thyself: I am the LORD.
> —Leviticus 19:18

And as repeated again in the New Testament:

> ***"Master, which is the great commandment in the law? Jesus said unto him 'Thou shalt love the Lord thy God with all thy heart, and with all thy soul, and with all thy mind.***
>
> ***This the first and great commandment. And the second is like unto it,***
>
> ***Thou shalt love thy neighbour as thyself.***
>
> ***On these two commandments hang all the law and the prophets."***
>
> —Matthew 22: 36-40

ASK everyone, all our cousins in the world to follow that one great law.

Successful Prayer

Hopefully you see now that the brain is the key to successful prayer, successful thinking. Mental images activate the same region of the brain that actual perception does. Praying, asking, thinking through direct attention can send focused vibrating thought through the pathways of the striatum in frontal cortex and connect further to the soul, the mind that some say is located deep in the brain. The microtubules and neurons process your "asks". Your brain and thought waves transmit them out to the Universe, the Universal Mind.

How can you do this? Would it help to pretend that your brain is truly a computer? Most people can visualize some of the circuitry in a computer. Wires, chips, microprocessors; key in some words, hit send, and zip—it is off into the wireless internet world letting your friend know you are thinking of them. They key in some words and send back *Thank you*. Zing! You have it back on your computer and you "see" it in your brain. Could this not be the same for a luminous human thought wave internet? Think of it as our own Universal Mind web.

How to compile the message, how to press send?

Visualize knocking on a door on your heart and watch it open, letting the energy of the emotion of love seep in and up to your brain. Perhaps visualize a climb up the ribs and spine. Step into the brain cavity; maybe there is a cushy chair for you to sit in. Find the keyboard to type your thoughts. Imagine, as you type, seeing the energy of the words, the mental imagery flowing through gateways into the networking circuitry of the coils of your brain. Is there someone there sitting beside you? Perhaps there is a strong energy force guiding you, helping your thoughts project. Key away, plan your day, plan your life, ASK… then press the send key.

What is your plan for today?

_____

_____

_____

Press send.

Empower your brain

Keep your brain healthy. It is a mass of fatty oil-filled tissue. Pictures show the brain to be kind of a gelatine-type blob yet crisscrossed with pattern after pattern of connective and communicating tissues. Time to start imagining what your brain looks like, what neuron conducting pathways there are in it. Understand how it operates, where to focus, to imagine your thoughts flowing and vibrating.

Even as I am typing right now, my brain is directing my thoughts to push impulses to nerves in my hands to hit the keys that I want to hit to form the words that I choose. It is not my liver that is doing this; it is my brain. Visualize your brain as the tool that is working for you.

The brain is the equipment that gets those microtubules working to tell the neurons in your muscles to work in your legs when you want to walk. The brain is what controls all of your body functions and its state of health.

However, it is YOUR consciousness, your soul, and the essence of you that controls what the brain tool does. Just as your brain operates your physical body, it operates what your conscious wants to show as emotions, as thought connections to others and to the outer world. Work with that to create a positive outcome for yourself and others.

ASK, BELIEVE, & RECEIVE

The book *Power Up Your Brain* by David Perlmutter M.D. and Alberto Villoldo PhD has some excellent advice on how to look after your brain and keep it healthy and stimulated.

Keep your brain healthy with oil supplements such as omega oil, olive oil and coconut oil. Add antioxidants like blueberry and broccoli, also available as capsules so that you don't have to eat pounds of broccoli.

Don't harm the brain with substances that will be detrimental to its proper functioning. Some substances considered not to be noxious actually harmfully adhere to the fatty tissues in your body. That would be your reproductive organs, and yes, your soft fatty brain tissues. The orbito-frontal cortex shrinks with continued substance usage; this is the decision making part of the brain. The brain rewires itself to compensate for the now smaller organ, causing the brain to work overtime to compensate. Functioning appears fine, but this connectivity does not appear to last in the long-term. These substances make you feel relaxed, but continued use over time can put you into a constant state of relaxation to the point that you may lose your ambition, your drive to succeed. You are happy but not going anywhere in life.

The times when your brain is not fully aware of the surroundings that your body is in, are the times that you can be most affected by the detrimental "thought vibrations" of others.

What are you going to do today to help your brain? Eat healthy? Get some good sleep? Go for a walk? Do a puzzle?

_____

_____

_____

_____

THE ANSWER: THOUGHTS ARE THINGS

It is your brain, it is your thinking power source; look after it! Stay in control of your life.

15.
GIVING THE ANSWER TO YOU TO TRY

The method that I am about to lay out is not meant to take away from anything you might now be doing to guide your life. In fact, if you are already writing your goals down and using vision boards that is great. They are a key component to guiding your conscious and unconscious thoughts.

Spiritual leaders have been known to sit and meditate for days to achieve "enlightenment". What I am going to lay out for you is a method that will add power to your thoughts, and possibly speed up the connection to enlightenment. Speed up the connection to your goals, your dreams, your connection to the Super Universal consciousness that just may be the Kingdom of God.

The lost gospel of Thomas says that the Kingdom is within us and all around us. So I've set out a pattern, a method on how to pray. I'm not claiming it to be the absolute and only method. I am saying it is a good working model. It sets the tone for relaxing, for quieting the mind, making it ready to receive your request.

Read through the next pages, and read through the suggested method a few times to prepare for doing it. It will become second nature as the framework to comprehensive thinking is built.

The steps are meant to bring to you the magnetic power of the science of "Thank you"—to give you a way "in" to the power of your brain by creating a neural framework, a neural pathway to higher cognitive processing through a pattern of praying, of asking, of thinking. This will focus your thoughts so that when they are sent to the Universe as electrical vibrating impulses, they will attract to you the reality that you want.

Write it down

Start by writing down all the things that you would like to happen in your world. I have shared samples of what I wrote down. Did everything I've ever written "happen"? No, but a lot did, some as mentioned previously in this book.

It is very important to write things down. Write down the date—it focuses your thoughts, puts your goals and plans on paper for you to read and refer to, and validates your successes.

The "Wow factor" happens when a prayer, an ask, is answered and you look back and realize that what you received was exactly what you had asked for. If it wasn't written down, you might think it was just chance that you were successful. You may not be sure whether you had "thought" that or not. If it is written down, there is no doubt, and it builds your confidence in the process.

So write stuff down. This starts the power of "the Thought" and "the Word". Write down your goals, your dreams for your work, your family, your life. Write them down without restriction. Do not limit your dreams by letting doubts in. Dream big and fall back only if you have to. Some people write down goals and toss the paper in a drawer. Years later, they find the paper and are amazed at the number of goals that have been reached even without focusing on them.

Here is some space to write down some key "Asks". Did you write a name of someone in need in the very first part of this book? Do you want to make a request for them?

THE ANSWER: THOUGHTS ARE THINGS

Visualize it
Imagine what can happen if you take some time to focus on your goals and your dreams—especially now that you know that your brain's quantum computer can be "asked" to help you connect with all possibilities, all realities.

The Energy fabric of the Universe, the Thinking Substance is there, and the power of connecting with God is within you. So in your writing, how specific were you? Look at what you have written and possibly re-write them again with more detail, or at least pick one to write out in detail. If you dream of a new house, describe the house. Is it a two-storey? How many bedrooms are there? What does the kitchen look like?

Can you visualize yourself walking from the kitchen into the living room? What does the furniture look like, where is the fireplace, and what is the view out the window? Did it get a bit more "real" for you? All that detail would certainly have gotten into your brain at the conscious level and deeper.

So take a minute to really put some detail into one or more of the top priority items and pick one that you want to focus on first. That is where we will apply your electrical "thinking".

Lots of writing, isn't it?

This might be where you would want to purchase a journal to write these in—just a simple bound booklet with lines to write on. Give it a title, such as "Hopes, Dreams, Thank you". Use vision boards, cut out pictures, and post them on a board or a piece of construction paper. The visualization augments your writing of the Word and more quickly sends the message to your subconscious to work on attracting.

Magnetise your Emotion

Now we have to increase the power level of Attraction. Increase your magnetic field. Increase your vibration bubble. What is your happy thought? Dig deep and find a memory, a person, a place, an event that brings an immense warm glow to you.

Conjure up a feeling of love, and attach that feeling to someone or to something so that when you bring the person or event to mind, you bring the "warm fuzzy" of that moment to you, right into the very present moment. Do you have a photo, a picture to stimulate that warm feeling?

Realistically, not everyone in the world is a happy camper. "Love" is not the top emotion for them. So maybe you can achieve the magnet of Emotion by being thankful. Gratitude, as I mentioned previously, and as many inspirational leaders say, is a huge and strong emotion. Even if life isn't totally great, you can be thankful for being alive. Give thanks for the sunshine, or for the snow.

Be thankful for being able to talk, or to listen, or to walk, or to sing. Some folks make their daily walks a gratitude walk. With every step they say *Thank you, thank you* to match their steps. *Thank you* to what they see around them while they walk. *Thank you* to the birds, the trees. *Thank you* for people that are in their lives. *Thank you* for the workers that built the roads and sidewalks. Practice mindful, meditative, prayer walking. Smile. Yes, even to smile evokes good emotion.

But "the greatest of these is Love", so try to find your "love" thought.

THE ANSWER: THOUGHTS ARE THINGS

Saying thank you, giving and receiving love, and offering smiles brings out emotion. Emotion is the magnet. So if you can triple this up by having one vision, one person, one musical tune that you can bring to mind that immediately brings love, thankfulness, gratitude, a surge of emotion, then you have your prayer tool, your ask tool.

What/where/who is your happy thought?

_____
_____
_____

Location, location, location—choose your place

How are we doing so far? We have our item from our list to think about, pray on, to ask on, and we have our emotional driver. Now, do you have a quiet spot in your home? If not, can you create one? Jesus said to pray in a closet. Now, I haven't tried that yet, but maybe I should. That might increase the power of the prayer.

Where is your calm spot?

_____
_____
_____

How about a comfortable chair in a quiet room? It probably should be away from the hustle and bustle of the household if possible. Perhaps if you are comfortable sitting on the floor, a nice big cushion would work. You might have to clear out a closet and stick a cushion in it! Let's start with a comfy chair.

Timing

Think of your spot, your chair, or your cushion as your thinking chair, your Prayer Chair. Now, find the time to pray. It can be hard to get a quiet spot in an active household. You may be an early riser. Perhaps an early morning would give you a half hour to sit, read, pray, ask and imagine.

At the opposite end of the scale, many inspirational leaders suggest to have this quiet time at the end of the day. Shut off all media or remove yourself from the noise of it all (using ear plugs if need be), and settle yourself in your spot.

The theory here is that what you last "think" and pray on will set the tone for your conscious and subconscious mind to "think" on and go to work on as you sleep. Some pray as they tuck themselves into bed. "Now I lay me down to sleep" is the first line of the children's bedtime prayer. Dr. Joseph Murphy's book suggested saying a powerful word, such as *wealth* or *success* over and over as you fall asleep. Add the word *happiness*.

Just because "you" are sleeping doesn't mean that your quantum computer like brain is sleeping, too. It continues to receive "electric" waves of energy from the greater universe of energy. If focused, your brain may be working on your request all night and transmitting out your thought waves.

You may already have had the experience of going to sleep with a problem weighing on your mind only to wake in the morning with the answer. How else could this be solved except by your brain? It has solved or received the answer somehow while "you" were sleeping.

Did you choose a time that will work best?

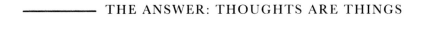 THE ANSWER: THOUGHTS ARE THINGS

Now, just read through the method below; this will walk you through your first prayer before following suit.

In the Beginning

To pray, you need to pull together the "thought", the "emotion", the "place" and the "time".

Settle in your spot, close your eyes, and start by breathing slowly and deeply. If it is hard to calm down, you can put on head phones and listen to softly played crystal singing bowls or Tibetan singing bowls. Classical instrumental music may work for you.

Louis Armstrong's "It's a Wonderful World" really hits a good chord with me and makes me smile right from the first notes. Count your breaths. Count breaths down from twenty down to one. In on twenty, and out, in on nineteen and out right on down. It is harder than you might think, as our brains are easily distracted. Maybe light a candle, or look into the flames of a fireplace if you have one. Lower your eyelids until they are almost closed. Think of it as focusing the light energy of the universe, or if it works for you, as the light of the Christ candle often lit in church services. You might have to start with shortening the count, breathing in on ten… nine… eight… seven… six… five… four… three… two… one.

Quiet your thoughts, bring calm into the moment, and then bring the emotion of your happy memory into the room with you, and into your mind. Take more deep slow breaths. Say *Thank you, thank you*, and *thank you* as you do your slow breathing.

Bring your hands into a prayerful formation, either outstretched and upward, resting lightly on your legs or clasped lightly in your lap, or palm to palm and held close to your forehead. Possibly position your clasped hands with your thumbs under your chin, with your first fingers on the bridge of your nose. Even touch your longest fingertips to that key spot between but just above your eyebrows. This will give you a real sense of closeness and connection to that wired up brain of yours. Look upward inside your closed eyelids.

Bow your head. You are about to ask your inner power and an Infinite Intelligent Power higher than your own to connect with you. It is good to ask respectfully. Smile.

You may have your own connection prayer. I use the Lord's Prayer in the Bible as suggested by Jesus. There is some variation around whether to use *forgive us our debts, our sins,* or *our trespasses*. Matthew 6:9-13 uses *debts* and *debtors*, and goes on to say in Matthew 6:14, "For if ye forgive men their trespasses, your heavenly Father will also forgive you." Luke 11:2-4 uses "forgive us our sin and forgive everyone that is indebted to us."

Note that both the Matthew and the Luke scripture in The Holy Bible Authorized King James Version say "Our Father, Which art in Heaven". How did so many bibles start to advocate to pray saying "Who art in Heaven"? Saying "Which" would allude to an essence and presence of the great I Am that is God. Saying "Who" infers a vision of a human looking God and may support the references to human beings "made in our image."

Perhaps even our Lord's prayer got "translated" for mankind.

The first time through, just say it as you normally would.

When finished, remember to say, *Thank you for today. Thank you for all my days.*

THE ANSWER: THOUGHTS ARE THINGS

Now pause. Let that sink in a bit. Slowly take two or three breaths more. Say/think *Thank you, thank you,* and *thank you.* Smile.

Now say the Lord's Prayer once more, only this time one phrase at a time. Think about each word. Tighten the skin on the back of your head to help you feel the words go into your brain, and hear them echo inside your skull. You want to physically feel the words if you can. Looking upward to one spot inside your eyelids you may get a sense of connecting with the eye of God or at least seeing a violet glow.

Our Father,

Which art

In Heaven,

Hallowed be

Thy name

Thy Kingdom

come.

Thy will

Be done

On Earth

As it is

In Heaven

Give us

This day

Our

ASK, BELIEVE, & RECEIVE

Daily bread

And

Forgive us

Our trespasses

As we

Forgive those

Who trespass

Against us

And lead us

Not

Into temptation

But

Deliver us

From evil.

For Thine

Is the Kingdom,

The Power

And the Glory,

Forever

And ever

Amen

THE ANSWER: THOUGHTS ARE THINGS

Infinite Intelligence, Creator God, Lord Jesus please I ASK that_____

I truly BELIEVE that_____

Others have received this; I believe that I can receive this also.

I RECEIVE this_____

With thankfulness; huge gratitude and Love. Thank you so much.

This I ASK, This I BELIEVE, This I RECEIVE!

Thank you, Thank you, Thank you, Thank you, Thank you.

Thank you Father for you have heard me, I know that you always hear me.

Amen. _____(your name)

Consider repeating this prayer daily, focusing on one thing for one week at a time. Do it in your brain chamber. Do quick prayers, "asks" throughout the day. Releasing it each time to the Universal Mind, telling your Conscious mind to direct your Subconscious mind to "attract" to you what you hope for. As you pray with your eyes closed, you may see an image of mauve, deep blue possibly, in the shape of an eye or pupil of an eye. It feels very connecting.

When you say the Lord's Prayer slowly instead of dashing through it, does each Word seem more meaningful? Circle one:

        Yes   No   Maybe

Therefore I say unto you, What things soever ye desire, when ye pray, believe that ye receive them, and ye shall have them.

—Mark 11:24

ASK, BELIEVE, & RECEIVE

Now that you have read over the method, are you ready for your first shot at it?

First prayer, First Ask

To make your future prayers as successful as possible, set the stage for success. After calming your world with your relaxation and Lord's Prayer, your first "Ask" could be as follows:

Creator God, Infinite Intelligence; Please, I ASK for the Power to help and heal myself and others. I ASK for the Power to attract health, wealth, happiness, success and love to myself and others.

I BELIEVE I have this Power because the Power of God was given to all mankind "made in His image" with a conscious powerful thinking brain.

There have been other healers and wise learned persons all throughout history. I too can be a Healer, a Savant with the Power to bring health, happiness, wealth, success and love for myself and others.

I RECEIVE the good news of having the Power to be healthy, happy, wealthy and successful with huge gratitude and thankfulness. I will use this Power to help myself and others to love and cherish life. Please bring this TO BE.

This I Ask, This I Believe, This I Receive, Thank you Lord, the Great I Am.

Thank you, Thank you, and Thank you. Thank you, Father, that you have heard me, for I know that you always hear me. Amen.

THE ANSWER: THOUGHTS ARE THINGS

This could be your focused prayer to start and occasionally after that. Praying it in your journal and praying it out loud and "Thinking" about it during the day. Imagine your new life!

You can pray other "asks" too, but this could be the starting point and the prayer to jump start everything.

How do you feel about asking for self-empowerment?

_____

_____

_____

Asking for personal Helping Power gives you confidence to think and ask for future positive outcomes.

Now, carry on making prayer and asking, as a constant habit in your life. Create that neural framework in your brain to connect with your higher cognitive thinking processes.

Did you pick a "thought" to focus on yet? Big ones can be successful; minor ones can be successful, too. Generally, your Life Path should turn out more as you would hope it would be by having a positive attitude, and through positive thinking.

Pull together the "thought", the "emotion", the "place" and the "time" and just get started writing in prayer, praying with both spoken and silent prayer and thinking.

Use tools that you find in the various Law of Attraction books. These writers have great and valid thoughts to try. But I truly believe that the final true door to attracting a better life, a better world, a better reality, a better vibration to you is through regular continuous prayer, continuous asking and continuous thinking.

Constant prayer, constant "asks", will create a neural framework and a direct pathway to communicating to your quantum computer brain, through your frontal cortex. Your brain will communicate with the greater Universe; with the super subconscious; the Infinite Intelligence and Universal mind of the Omnipresent God.

My friend Jan asked, "Why would the Bible say 'Pray without ceasing'?" The origin of the word *pray* is "to ask". The Bible is telling all of us to ask without ceasing, to think constantly, to engage in strong, focused thinking, and in focused asking. That is the Pathway we are to follow. **PROGRAM YOUR BRAIN.**

Nothing that I am suggesting you to try should take you away from your current beliefs or current religion if you do participate in one. This should only strengthen your faith, your knowledge, and communication with the higher power of Infinite Knowledge that is there to guide you (along with the angels that are there to help you). As Plato said, for mankind to "know something", that which is known must be unchanging; there must be genuine knowledge that does not change. Infinite Knowledge, Universal Mind.

After a week, try another "ask". Do not despair if things aren't instant. Some things take time to cohere together to create the reality that you are seeking. I had visualized a new church building for our congregation. It took a couple of years but it is in process now. I hope you are pleasantly surprised by the number of successes you have.

Science today is proving more and more that our brains contain a computer-like component and computers contain brain-like components. The Higgs Boson God-particle is now an actual term used in reference to research into the big bang event that was the start of the universe and possible starter of life. Nobel laureate Leon Lederman used the term God-particle because discovery of that particle could unify understanding of particle physics and help humans "know the mind of God".

The internet is now a common place communication tool, a huge "cloud" of easily accessible knowledge. The concept of such a thing was unheard of only a short time ago.

More and more is being revealed of ancient beliefs, ancient learnings about drawing strength and power from the energy around us. We each could truly have a luminous "web" of energy, knowledge and thoughts surrounding us. Our thought webs could be part of a worldwide luminous web of energy, knowledge and thoughts.

We simply have to capture the skill to manage our thoughts using the essence that is ourselves, our soul, our conscious. Understand the functioning of your brain so that your essence, your soul can direct the brain's subconscious thinking power—that power to not just survive but to thrive.

How do you plan on directing your sub consciousness? What do you want to attract? It does not have to be a "thing"; it can be peace of mind or calmness of spirit, time to think:

_____

_____

_____

16.
ASK, BELIEVE, RECEIVE

I propose to you now that God is a verb. God is the action word YHWH, and no matter how we might struggle to pronounce it, it is the Word, and the Word means I AM, TO EXIST. We pray to a "Father Which art in heaven", not to Who art in heaven. God is the vibrating energy that exists all around us and in us; that Light is a wave until we see it, until we attract it to us. Then that Light wave becomes a Particle. The vibrating Light and the vibrating Energy keep the shape of the vibrating Particle as we imagined it, as we *Thought* it to be, as we or nature has observed it and brought it TO BE.

Whether you believe that the unpronounceable YHWH is the original name of God, to be spoken or not spoken; it does refer to the Great I Am; and I Am to Be. It could truly be a verb as indicated by research and mean TO BE, TO EXIST, TO LIVE. We exist in the living thinking substance, the energy of YHWH.

The glowing counsellor behind the oak screen in my personal group of counsellors is the Light of my guardian angel, always with me to guide and protect me. Yes, it is one of those shimmering, luminescent, singing, loving orb beings that I searched for, imagined, and found through deep loving thought. Remember that a wave of light becomes a particle when "observed". Perhaps imagination becomes a thing when it is thought about. Look after your brain; it has the thinking power to influence your life. That is the Answer. There is a Power in The spoken Word, The Way and The Light.

Keep reading, keep learning, and keep seeking knowledge. Humans were always meant to seek, to harness goodness and light through our thoughts. The pathway, the Answer, has been laid out for us for thousands of years. All those ancient myths, stories and gospels were collected and passed on to lead us to knowledge, thinking and power, particularly in the words of the prophets, and especially the actual words of the first-born son of God called Jesus.

USE THE POWER OF YOUR BRAIN TO ASK, BELIEVE and RECEIVE.

This IS the Answer to how human kind survives. We do LIVE the reality created by our own vibrating thoughts, by our own "asking"; with the help of our own powerful brains given to us by the Infinite Universal Intelligence, the Great Omnipresent Divinity that we are part of. The vibrating thinking substance is the Kingdom that is all around us in that space that is empty space. With each breath we take, we draw in that thinking substance "TO BE the best we can be". Draw in that vibrating energy power.

And yes; our wired up connected neuron branches in our thinking brains do help us ASK in some way.

Henry Ford was the inventor of the first Ford vehicle and the patriarch of the Ford dynasty. One of his quotes went something like this:

>If you think you can, you will.

>If you think you can't, you will not.

States it quite clearly, doesn't it?

THE ANSWER: THOUGHTS ARE THINGS

Here is another creed that you might find inspirational. Martin was a respected member of our community and local church. He lived by the following saying that has its roots in the fifth century and encouraged others to also do so. This is his version of the creed.

> Look to this day, for it is life
>
> For yesterday is but a dream,
>
> And tomorrow is only a vision.
>
> But today, well lived,
>
> Makes every yesterday
>
> A dream of happiness.
>
> And every tomorrow
>
> A vision of hope.
>
> Look well, therefore,
>
> ...to this day...

You cannot change the past—it is in the past. Plan the future that is yet to come. Live well today, in the power of Now.

What YOU are living today was formed by what your brain has thought of up to (and including) today.

Focus on the Reality, the Future that YOU want.

ASK without ceasing. Thoughts are indeed vibrational Things! Thoughts are truly the ultimate energy currency. Watch what you think and say! In the beginning was the spoken Word ...and the Word was made flesh....

ASK... BELIEVE... RECEIVE!

Will you try to seek the Answer and try to Think your way to a better life for yourself? Circle one:

        Yes   No   Maybe

THE END

END NOTES

1.) All biblical quotes in this book are from The Holy Bible Authorized King James Version, Bible House, Charlotte-North Carolina printed in USA unless otherwise referenced.

2.) The Living Bible Paraphrased 1971 Tyndale House Publishers, Wheaton, Illinois ISBN 0-8326-1415-7 Concordance

3.) Divinity is within you – ancient Hindu saying, thousands of years old - Public Domain

4.) Seek Ye First. Matthew 6:33 by Leon O. Poole - Public Domain [Copy Freely]

5.) Thoughts are Things & the Real and the Unreal, The Collected "New Thought" Wisdom of Prentice Mulford and Charles Fillmore.

Published: November 2011 (Paperback and Kindle); Limitless Press LLC, Jupiter Fl. The works reproduced in this book are understood to be in the public domain and no longer subject to copyright laws. No copyright is sought or claimed on these works. Original text was compiled from free sources.

6.) Alexander M.D., Eben. *Proof of Heaven*, 2012 Simon and Schuster Paperbacks, a division of Simon & Schuster Inc. New York

READING LIST

Allan, James. *As A Man Thinketh.* New York: Penguin Group, 1903, 2008

Batto, Bernard F. *Slaying the Dragon, Mythmaking in the Biblical Tradition.* Louisville, Kentucky. Westminster John Knox Press. 1992)

Blenkinsopp, Joseph. *Human Origins, Genesis 1:1-11:26, The Pentateuch, An Introduction to the First Five Books of the Bible.* New York. Double Day. 1992

Byrne, Rhonda. *The Secret.* New York: Simon & Schuster Inc., 2006

Butterfield, Eric. *Discover the Power Within You.* New York: Harper Collins, 1968, 1992

Canfield, Jack. *Key to Living the Law of Attraction.* Deerfield Beach: Health Communications, 2007

Collier, Robert. *Riches Within Your Reach.* New York: Penguin Group, 1947, 2009

Collier, Robert. *The Secret of the Ages.* New York: Penguin Group, 1926, 1947, 2007

Covey, Stephen R. *The 7 Habits of Highly Effective People.* New York: Simon & Shuster, 1989

Eker, T. Harv. *Secrets of the Millionaire Mind.* New York: Harper Collins, 2005

Fillmore, Cora & Charles. *Teach Us To Pray.* Missouri: Unity Books.1941, 2002, 2011

Graves, Robert & Patai, Raphael. *The Fall of Man, Hebrew Myths: the Book of Genesis.* New York. Greenwich House. 1983 reprint of 1963, 1964 edition)

Greene, Brian R. *The Elegant Universe.* New York: W.W Norton & Company. 1999, 2003

Haanel, Charles F. *The Master Key System.* New York: Penguin Group, 1917, 2007

Hameroff, Stuart. *Ultimate Computing* 1987

Hebb, Donald O. *The Organization of Behavior.* New York: Wiley & Sons, 1949

Hill, Napoleon. *Think and Grow Rich.* New York: Penguin Group, 1937, 2005

Polkinghorne, John *Quarks, Chaos & Christianity.* New York: Crossroad. 1994, 2005

Losier, Michael J. *Law of Attraction, The Science of Attracting More of What You Want and Less of What you Don't.* New York: Hatchette Books, 2010

Murphy, Dr. Joseph. *The Power of Your Subconscious Mind.* New York: Bantam, 1982, 2000

Nelson, Dwight K. *Built to Last, Creation & Evolution: A thoughtful look at the evidence that a Master Designer created our planet.* Oshawa, Ontario: Idaho Pacific Press, 1998

Norville, Deborah. *How the New Science of Thank you can change your Life, adapted from Thank You Power.* Readers Digest: October, 2008

Penrose, Roger, *Shadows of the Mind: A Search for the Missing Science of Consciousness,* Oxford: 1994. This discusses the Orch-OR theory.

Perlmutter, Dr. David & Villoldo, Dr. Alberto. *Power Up Your Brain The Neuroscience of Enlightenment.* Vancouver: Hay House, 2010

Schwartz, M.D. Jeffrey M., and Sharon Begley *The Mind & The Brain, Neuroplasticity and the Power of Mental Force,* 2002. HarperCollins Publishers New York

Taylor, Rev. Barbara Brown. *An Alter in the World.* New York: Harper Collins, 2009

Taylor, Rev. Barbara Brown. *The Luminous Web.* Cambridge: Cowley Productions, 2000

Taylor, Dr. Travis. *The Science Behind the Secret.* New York: Simon & Shuster, 2010

Tolle, Elkhart. *The Power of Now.* Vancouver. Namaste Publishing: 1999, 2004

Virtue, Doreen. *Angel Numbers 101.* Vancouver: Raincoast, 2008

Vitale, Joe. *The Key.* 2007 www.mrfire.com

Wattles, Wallace. *The New Science of Getting Rich.* New York: Simon & Shuster, 1910, 2007

APPENDIX I

"Holy Bookscom" is a large collection of high quality sacred texts, holy books, and spiritual texts as PDF ebooks, that you will find on the Internet. All books are free to down load, all books are Free Public Domain Books. The Gospel Thomas is listed here as a public domain book. There are translations that might not be in the public domain. The intent in offering information on the book here is to encourage interested readers to research and read the entire gospel.

The Gospel According to Thomas was found in Egypt in 1945, only available for our reading in the last 100 years but was actually written close to 2000 years ago. These are direct citations of Jesus Christ in 114 verses believed to be written prior to the year 340 in Coptic.

This gospel is written in parables similar to the canonical New Testament gospels. Translation can vary and can change the understanding. Originally translated as Coptic and Greek translations, and then into English and more. Here is an example of the Saying 3) of Thomas's gospel translated in Coptic, Greek and in the New Testament.

Coptic 3) Jesus said, "If those *who lead* you say, 'Look, the Realm is in the sky,' then the birds of the sky will precede you. If they say to you, 'It is *in the sea*,' then the fish will precede you. *Rather,* **the Realm is inside of you and outside of you. When you come to know yourselves,** *then you will become known,* **and you will realize that it is you who are the children of the living Father.** But if you will not know yourselves, you live in poverty and it is you yourselves who are that poverty."

Greek 3) Jesus said, "If those *pulling* you say, 'Look! The Realm is in the sky,' then the birds of the sky will precede you, or if they say to you, 'It is *under the earth*,' then the fish of the sea will precede you. **The Realm of God is inside you and outside you. Those who know themselves will find it; and *when you know yourselves,* you will know that you are children of the living Father**. But if you will not know yourselves, you are in poverty and you are the poverty."

New Testament Luke 17:20 – 21) Once Jesus was asked by the Pharisees when God's Realm would come. Jesus said, "God's Realm won't come just because you're watching for it, and neither can people say, 'Here it is!' or 'There it is', because **God's Realm is actually within you!"**

Slightly different wording in the three, but the main theme is there in each one: **"God's Realm is actually within you"**.

The Text of the Gospel of Thomas - excerpts

These are the secret sayings that the living Jesus spoke and Didymos Judas Thomas recorded.

> Saying 113) His disciples said to him, ***"When will the (Father's) imperial rule come?" "It will not come by watching for it. It will not be said, 'Look, here!' or 'Look, there!' 'Rather, the Father's imperial rule is spread out upon the earth, and people don't see it."***
>
> Saying 114) Simon Peter said to them, "Make Mary leave us, for females don't deserve life." Jesus said, ***"Look, I will guide her to make her male, so that she too may become a living spirit resembling you males. For every female who***

__makes herself male will enter the domain of Heaven."__]

THE GOSPEL OF THOMAS Translations by: Thomas O. Lambdin (Coptic version); B.P Grenfell & A.S. Hunt (Greek Fragments); Bentley Layton (Greek Fragments); Commentary by: Craig Schenk - Had this comment on the Gospel of Thomas:

["The Sayings are not intended to be interpreted literally, as their New Testament parallels often are, but to be interpreted symbolically, as attested by Saying #1. While a literal interpretation may make sense; only by understanding the deeper meanings of the Sayings can one truly understand them. Thus in Saying #114, it is to be understood that "male" symbolizes the pneumatic (Spiritual or Gnostic) Christians and "female" symbolizes the psychic (unenlightened, or orthodox) Christians, rather than actually referring to males and females.]

True understanding of these texts is meant to come from personal contact with the Divine Inspiration from within.

APPENDIX II

The Lost Gospel of Peter (c. 70-150 AD) is of public domain, being 2,000 years old and can be found at http://www.sacred-texts.com/. The site indicates that people are free to photocopy or circulate this gospel of Peter in any way they desire.

In the valley of the Upper Nile, on the right bank of the river, is the town of Akhmîm Panopolis of ancient times with monasteries and temple ruins.

In 1888, while excavating the grave of a monk a French archaeological mission discovered a parchment codex. Translation proved it to be a portion of The Gospel According to Peter.

The world changed dramatically in the nineteen centuries in which the parchment lay in the tomb preserving ancient scriptures documenting a most momentous historical event.

The gospel was not unheard of as it was referred to by Bishops in 190 AD and 300 AD; and by historians in 253 AD; and 455 AD. Scholars knew the document existed but it was lost to mankind for a long time.

Of the twenty-nine variations between the Lost Gospel According to Peter and the New Testament canonical gospels the most notable differences are:

1. Who gave the order for the execution — Herod.

2. Pilate's friend was Joseph.

3. There was a darkness following the crucifixion in which many went about with lamps and fell down.

4. Our Lord's cry of "My power, my power"; not "My God, my God".

5. The disciples hid because they were searched for as malefactors that may want to burn the temple.

6. Petronius was the centurion who kept watch at the tomb.

7. The resurrection and the ascension occurred on the same day.

This Gospel of Peter was once as highly honoured as the Gospels of Matthew, Mark, Luke and John. Peter often showed leadership in the group of Twelve Apostles and was close to Jesus. As one of the close confidantes his Gospel and that of Apostle Thomas should have been selected for the Bible publication for all to ponder.

APPENDIX III

The Nag Hammadi Library - The Sophia of Jesus Christ (c.50-200 AD)

Translated by Douglas M. Parrott - Archive Note

The translation of "The Sophia of Jesus Christ" (also sometimes titled, "The Wisdom of Jesus Christ") is derived from two separately preserved copies of the text. The first copy is in Nag Hammadi Codex III (NHC III); a second copy of this text was preserved in the Berlin Gnostic Codex. A third fragment of the text in Greek was also found among the Oxyrhynchus papyrus documents.] Oxyrhynchus being a city in Upper Egypt where many well preserved ancient documents have been excavated.

Thus we have three distinct copies of this scripture attested from three separate ancient sources, two in Coptic, one in Greek. (Again our three newspapers reporting on one subject)

The Sophia of Jesus Christ - From Wikipedia, the free encyclopedia

The Sophia of Jesus Christ is one of many Gnostic writings from the Nag Hammadi codices, discovered in Egypt in 1945. The Coptic manuscript itself has been dated to the 4th century; however, it is complemented by a few fragments in Greek dating from the 3rd century, implying an earlier date.

Highly mystical, the content of this text concerns creation of gods, angels, and the universe with an emphasis on infinite and metaphysical truth.

The perfect Saviour hath said: "Come (you) from things unseen unto the end of those that are seen, and the very emanation of Thought shall reveal unto you how faith in they which are unseen was found in them which are seen, they that belong to the Unbegotten Father. Whom so ever hath ears to hear, let him hear!" - From The Sophia of Jesus Christ

The text is composed of 13 questions from the disciples, followed by brief discourses by Jesus in response.

The questions concern:

- the vanity and futility of searching for God.
- how to find truth, but only explaining what it is not.
- how truth was revealed to the Gnostics (knowledge seekers) at the beginning of time.
- how one must awake to see the truth.
- how things began.
- how mankind came to gnosis.
- the position of Jesus in all this.
- the identity of Jesus.
- how the spirit connects to the material.
- the number of spirits.
- the immortal.
- those who are not material.
- where mankind came from and what purpose it should have.

Excerpt from The Sophia of Christ:

THE ANSWER: THOUGHTS ARE THINGS

"Then Thomas said to him: "Lord, Savior, how many are the aeons of those who surpass the heavens?"

The perfect Savior said: *"I praise you (pl.) because you ask about the great aeons, for your roots are in the infinities.*

The perfect Savior said: *"Whoever has ears to hear, let him hear. The first aeon is that of Son of Man, who is called 'First Begetter', who is called 'Savior', who has appeared.*

And all natures, starting from the revelation of chaos, are in the Light that shines without shadow, and joy that cannot be described, and unutterable jubilation. They ever delight themselves on account of their unchanging glory and the immeasurable rest, which cannot be described among all the aeons that came to be afterward, and all their powers.

Now all that I have just said to you, I said that you might shine in Light more than these."

I have given you authority over all things as Sons of Light, that you might tread upon their power with your feet."

These are the things the blessed Savior said, and he disappeared from them. Then all the disciples were in great, ineffable joy in the spirit from that day on. And his disciples began to preach the Gospel of God, the eternal, imperishable Spirit. Amen."

The text has strong similarities to the Epistle of Eugnostos (Eugnostos The Blessed) c.50-150 AD, which was also found in the Nag Hammadi codices, but the Sophia of Christ has a Christian framing added, expanding it somewhat.

APPENDIX IV

BIBLICAL WRITINGS:

Be enlightened. Read all of the words of Jesus from the common Bible and his spoken words as written in the many biblical writings and gospels from prior to Jesus' birth to 325 AD. There is a lifetime of reading material here that is available on the internet.

Chronological Listing of Biblical Writings – (B) indicates the 27 that were included in the King James Version of the Bible

Year (AD)	Biblical Writing
1. 30-60	Passion Narrative
2. 40-80	Lost Sayings Gospel Q
3. 50-60 (B)-7	1 Corinthians
4. 50-60 (B)-8	2 Corinthians
5. 50-60 (B)-9	Galatians
6. 50-60 (B)-11	Philippians
7. 50-60 (B)-13	1 Thessalonians
8. 50-60 (B)-6	Romans
9. 50-60 (B)-18	Philemon
10. 50-80 (B)-12	Colossians
11. 50-90	Signs Gospel
12. 50-95 (B)-19	Book of Hebrews

13.	50-120	Didache
14.	50-140	Gospel of Thomas
15.	50-140	Oxyrhynchus 1224 Gospel
16.	50-150	Apocalypse of Adam
17.	50-150	Eugnostos the Blessed
18.	50-200	Sophia of Jesus Christ
19.	65-80 (B)-2	Gospel of Mark
20.	70-100 (B)-20	Epistle of James
21.	70-120	Egerton Gospel
22.	70-160	Gospel of Peter
23.	70-160	Secret Mark
24.	70-200	Fayyum Fragment
25.	70-200	Testaments of the Twelve Patriarchs
26.	73-200	Mara Bar Serapion
27.	80-100 (B)-1	Gospel of Matthew
28.	80-100 (B)-10	1 Ephesians
29.	80-100 (B)-14	2 Thessalonians
30.	80-110 (B)-21	1 Peter
31.	80-120	Epistle of Barnabas
32.	80-130 (B)-3	Gospel of Luke
33.	80-130 (B)-5	Acts of the Apostles

34.	80-140	1 Clement
35.	80-150	Gospel of the Egyptians
36.	80-150	Gospel of the Hebrews
37.	80-250	Christian Sibyllines
38.	90-95 (B)-27	Apocalypse of John
39.	90-120 (B)-4	Gospel of John
40.	90-120 (B)-23	1 John
41.	90-120 (B)-24	2 John
42.	90-120 (B)-25	3 John
43.	90-120 (B)-26	Epistle of Jude
44.	93	Flavius Josephus
45.	100-150(B)-15	1 Timothy
46.	100-150 (B)-16	2 Timothy
47.	100-150 (B)-17	Titus
48.	100-150	Apocalypse of Peter
49.	100-150	Secret Book of James
50.	100-150	Preaching of Peter
51.	100-160	Gospel of the Ebionites
52.	100-160	Gospel of the Nazoreans
53.	100-160	Shepherd of Hermas
54.	100-160 (B)-22	2 Peter

55.	100-200	Odes of Solomon
56.	100-200	Gospel of Eve
57.	100-230	Thunder, Perfect Mind
58.	101-220	Book of Elchasai
59.	105-115	Ignatius of Antioch
60.	110-140	Polycarp to the Philippians
61.	110-140	Papias
62.	110-160	Oxyrhynchus 840 Gospel
63.	110-160	Traditions of Matthias
64.	111-112	Pliny the Younger
65.	115	Suetonius
66.	115	Tacitus
67.	120-130	Quadratus of Athens
68.	120-130	Apology of Aristides
69.	120-140	Basilides
70.	120-140	Naassene Fragment
71.	120-160	Valentinus
72.	120-180	Apocryphon of John
73.	120-180	Gospel of Mary
74.	120-180	Dialogue of the Savior
75.	120-180	Gospel of the Savior

76.	120-180	2nd Apocalypse of James
77.	120-180	Trimorphic Protennoia
78.	120-180	Gospel of Perfection
79.	120-200	Genna Marias
80.	130-140	Marcion
81.	130-150	Aristo of Pella
82.	130-160	Epiphanes On Righteousness
83.	130-160	Ophite Diagrams
84.	130-160	2 Clement
85.	130-170	Gospel of Judas
86.	130-200	Epistle of Mathetes to Diognetus
87.	140-150	Epistula Apostolorum
88.	140-160	Ptolemy
89.	140-160	Isidore
90.	140-170	Fronto
91.	140-170	Infancy Gospel of James
92.	140-170	Infancy Gospel of Thomas
93.	140-180	Gospel of Truth
94.	150-160	Martyrdom of Polycarp
95.	150-160	Justin Martyr
96.	150-180	Excerpts of Theodotus

97.	150-180	Heracleon
98.	150-200	Ascension of Isaiah
99.	150-200	Interpretation of Knowledge
100.	150-200	Testimony of Truth
101.	150-200	Acts of Peter
102.	150-200	Acts of John
103.	150-200	Acts of Paul
104.	150-200	Acts of Andrew
105.	150-225	Acts of Peter and the Twelve
106.	150-225	Book of Thomas the Contender
107.	150-250	Paraphrase of Shem
108.	150-250	Fifth and Sixth Books of Esra
109.	150-300	Authoritative Teaching
110.	150-300	Coptic Apocalypse of Paul
111.	150-300	Prayer of the Apostle Paul
112.	150-300	Discourse on the Eighth and Ninth
113.	150-300	Melchizedek
114.	150-350	Preaching of Paul
115.	150-350	Epistle to the Laodiceans
116.	150-350	Questions of Mary
117.	150-350	Allogenes, the Stranger

118.	150-350	Hypsiphrone
119.	150-350	Valentinian Exposition
120.	150-350	Act of Peter
121.	150-360	Concept of Our Great Power
122.	150-400	Acts of Pilate
123.	150-400	Anti-Marcionite Prologues
124.	150-400	Dialogue Between John and Jesus
125.	160-170	Tatian's Address to the Greeks
126.	160-180	Claudius Apollinaris
127.	160-180	Apelles
128.	160-180	Julius Cassianus
129.	160-250	Octavius of Minucius Felix
130.	161-180	Acts of Carpus
131.	165-175	Melito of Sardis
132.	165-175	Hegesippus
133.	165-175	Dionysius of Corinth
134.	165-175	Lucian of Samosata
135.	167	Marcus Aurelius
136.	170-175	Diatessaron
137.	170-200	Dura-Europos Gospel Harmony
138.	170-200	Muratorian Canon

139.	170-200	Treatise on the Resurrection
140.	170-220	Letter of Peter to Philip
141.	170-230	Thought of Norea
142	175-180	Athenagoras of Athens
143	175-185	Irenaeus of Lyons
144	175-185	Rhodon
145	175-185	Theophilus of Caesarea
146	175-190	Galen
147	178	Celsus
148	178	Letter from Vienna and Lyons
149	180	Passion of the Scillitan Martyrs
150	180-185	Theophilus of Antioch
151	180-185	Acts of Apollonius
152	180-220	Bardesanes
153	180-220	Kerygmata Petrou
154	180-230	Hippolytus of Rome
155	180-230	Sentences of Sextus
156	180-250	1st Apocalypse of James
157	180-250	Gospel of Philip
158	182-202	Clement of Alexandria
159	185-195	Maximus of Jerusalem

160	185-195	Polycrates of Ephesus
161	188-217	Talmud
162	189-199	Victor I
163	190-210	Pantaenus
164	190-230	Second Discourse of Great Seth
165	193	Anonymous Anti-Montanist
166	193-216	Inscription of Abercius
167	197-220	Tertullian
168	200-210	Serapion of Antioch
169	200-210	Apollonius
170	200-220	Caius
171	200-220	Philostratus
172	200-225	Acts of Thomas
173	200-230	Ammonius of Alexandria
174	200-230	Zostrianos
175	200-230	Three Steles of Seth
176	200-230	Exegesis on the Soul
177	200-250	Didascalia
178	200-250	Books of Jeu
179	200-300	Pistis Sophia
180	200-300	Tripartite Tractate

181	200-300	Hypostasis of the Archons
182	200-300	Prayer of Thanksgiving
183	200-300	Coptic Apocalypse of Peter
184	200-330	Apostolic Church Order
185	200-350	Holy Book of the Great Invisible Spirit
186	200-450	Monarchian Prologues
187	203	Acts of Perpetua and Felicitas
188	203-250	Origen
189	210-245	Lucian of Antioch
190	217-222	Callistus
191	230-265	Dionysius of Alexandria
192	230-268	Firmilian of Caesarea
193	240-260	Commodian
194	246-258	Cyprian
195	250-274	Gospel of Mani
196	250-300	Teachings of Silvanus
197	250-300	Excerpt from the Perfect Discourse
198	250-350	Coptic Apocalypse of Elijah
199	250-400	Apocalypse of Paul
200	251-253	Pope Cornelius
201	251-258	Novatian

202	254-257	Pope Stephen
203	259-268	Dionysius of Rome
204	260-280	Theognostus
205	265-282	Gregory Thaumaturgus
206	269-274	Pope Felix
207	270-310	Victorinus of Pettau
208	270-312	Methodius
209	270-330	Marsanes
210	270-330	On the Origin of the World
211	270-350	De Recta in Deum Fide
212	280-300	Hesychius
213	280-310	Pierius
214	280-310	Pamphilus of Caesarea
215	297-310	Arnobius of Sicca
216	300-311	Peter of Alexandria
217	300-320	Pseudo-Clementine Homilies
218	300-340	Eusebius of Caesarea
219	300-350	Manichean Acts of Leucius Charinus
220	300-390	Letters of Paul and Seneca
221	300-400	Apocalypse of Thomas
222	300-400	Freer Logion

223 300-600   Gospel of Gamaliel

224 303-316   Lactantius

225 310-334   Reticius of Autun

226 320-380   Pseudo-Clementine Recognitions

APPENDIX V

Excerpts from Thoughts Are Things – Prentice Mulford 1834-1891 is inserted here to make available to more people this information.

Thoughts are Things & the Real and the Unreal, The Collected "New Thought" Wisdom of Prentice Mulford and Charles Fillmore.

Published: November 2011 (Paperback and Kindle) Limitless Press LLC, Jupiter Fl. The works reproduced in this book are understood to be in the public domain and no longer subject to copyright laws. No copyright is sought or claimed on these works. Original text was compiled from free sources.

Chapter One- THE MATERIAL MIND V. THE SPIRITUAL MIND

THERE belongs to every human being a higher self and a lower self or mind of the spirit which has been growing for ages, and a self of the body, which is but a thing of yesterday. The higher self is full of prompting idea, suggestion and aspiration. This it receives of the Supreme Power.... The higher self argues possibilities and power for us greater than men and women now possess and enjoy....The higher self craves freedom from the cumbrousness, the limitations, the pains and disabilities of the body....The higher self wants a standard for right and wrong of its own. The lower self says we must accept a standard made for us by others--by general and long-held opinion, belief and prejudice...

This ever-acting, ever-varying force, which lies behind and, in a sense, creates all forms of matter we call Spirit.

To see, reason and judge of life and things in the knowledge of this force makes what is termed the "Spiritual Mind"

We have through knowledge the wonderful power of using or directing this force, when we recognize it, and know that it exists so as to bring us health, happiness and eternal peace of mind. Composed as we are of this force, we are ever attracting more of it to use and making it a part of our being.

With more of this force there must come more and more knowledge. At first in our physical existences we allow it to work blindly. Then we are in the ignorance of that condition known as the material mind….. as mind through growth or increase of this power becomes more and more awakened…

The spiritual mind will know it time that your thought influences people for or against your interests, though their bodies are thousands of miles distant. The material mind does not regard its thought as an actual element as real as air or water. The spiritual mind knows that every one of its thousand daily secret thoughts are real things acting on the minds of the persons they are sent to.

The spiritual mind knows that matter or the material is only an expression of spirit or force; that such matter is ever changing in accordance with the spirit that makes or externalizes itself in the form we call matter, and therefore, if the thought of health, strength and recuperation is constantly held to in the mind, such thought of health, strength and rejuvenation will express itself in the body, making maturity never ceasing, vigour never ending, and the keenness of every physical sense ever increasing…..

The higher mind or mind of the spirit knows that it possesses other senses akin to those of physical sight and hearing, but more powerful and far reaching…

…The spiritual mind, or mind opened to higher and newer forces of life, teaches that there is a law regulating the exercise of every physical sense. When we learn and follow this law, our gratifications and possessions do not prove sources of greater pain than happiness, as they do to so many.

THE ANSWER: THOUGHTS ARE THINGS

By the spiritual mind is meant a clearer mental sight of things and forces existing both in us and the Universe, and of which the race for the most part has been in total ignorance. We have now but a glimpse of these forces, those of some relatively a little clearer than those of others....

To Say a thing must be, is the very power that makes it... The spiritual or more enlightened mind says: If you would help to drive away sickness, turn your thought as much as you can on health, strength and vigour, and on strong, healthy, vigorous material things, such as moving clouds, fresh breezes, the cascade, the ocean surge; on woodland scenes and growing healthy trees; on birds full of life and motion; for in so doing you turn yourself into a real current or this healthy life-giving thought, which is suggested and brought you by the thought of such vigorous material objects.

And above all, try to rely and trust the Supreme Power which formed all these things and far more and which is the endless and inexhaustible part of your higher self or spiritual mind, and as your faith increases in this Power, so will your own power ever increase....

....when the spiritual mind has once commenced to awaken; nothing can stop its further waking, though the material may for a time retard it...

The condition of mind to be desired is the entire dominancy of the spiritual mind... implies the state of mind when the body will gladly lend its cooperation to all the desires of the spiritual mind.

Then all power can be given to your spirit. Then no force need be expended in resisting the hostility of the material mind. Then all such force will be used to further undertakings, to bring us material goods, to raise us higher and higher into realms of power, peace and happiness, to accomplish what now would be called miracles...

> ***"Holiness" implies wholeness, or whole action of the spirit on the body, or perfect control by your spirit over body, through knowledge and faith in our capacity to draw***

ever more and more from the Supreme Power...

When the material mind is put away, or, in other words, then we become convinced of the external existence of these spiritual forces, both in ourselves, and outside of ourselves, and when we learn to use them rightly (for we are now and always have been using them in some way). Then to use the words of Paul: "Faith is swallowed up in victory," and the sting and fear of death is removed.

Life becomes then one glorious advance forward from the pleasure of today to the greater pleasure of tomorrow, and the phrase "to live" means to enjoy.

In Chapter I Mulford is setting the stage that there are two parts to the brain, given many contrasting statements of what he called the Spiritual Mind (Higher Self) and Material Mind (Lower Self). He describes the Material Mind as accepting life as it comes, not believing there is more and the Spiritual Mind as rising up to Believe and Achieve more. The description is somewhat in line with what we refer today as the Subconscious Mind and Conscious Mind.

Chapter Three - THOUGHT CURRENTS

WE need to be careful of what we think and talk. Because thought runs in currents as real as those of air and water. Of what we think and talk we attract to us like current of thought. This acts on mind or body for good or ill.

If thought was visible to the physical eye we should see its currents flowing to and from people. We should see that persons similar in temperament, character and motive are in the same literal current of thought.

...and that each one in such moods serves as an additional battery or generator of such thought and is strengthening that particular element. We should see

THE ANSWER: THOUGHTS ARE THINGS

these forces working in similar manner and connecting the hopeful, courageous and cheerful, with all others hopeful, courageous and cheerful.

When you are low in spirits or "blue" you have acting on you the thought current coming from all others in low spirits.

In attracting to us the current of any kind of evil, we become for a time one with evil. In the thought current of the Supreme Power for good we may become more and more as one with that power, or in Biblical phrase "One with God." That is the desirable thought current for us to attract.

We have said in other books that "Talk Creates Force," and that the more who talk in sympathy the greater is the volume and power of the thought current generated and attracted for good or ill.

If but two people were to meet at regular intervals and talk of health, strength and vigour of body and mind, at the same time opening their minds to receive of the Supreme the best idea as to the ways and means for securing these blessings, they would attract to them a thought current of such idea.

If these two people or more kept up these conversations on these subjects at a regular time and place and found pleasure in such communing…they would be astonished at the year's end at the beneficial results to mind and body. Because in so doing and coming together with a silent demand of the Supreme to get the best idea, they would attract to them a current of the Life-giving force.

Let us endeavour, then, with the help of the Supreme Power, to get into the thought current of things that are healthy, natural, strong and beautiful.

We can more and more invite the thought current of things that are lively, sprightly and amusing. Life should be full of playfulness. Continued seriousness is but a few degrees removed from gloom and melancholy. Thousands live too much in the thought current of seriousness. Faces which wear a smiling expression are scarce. Some never smile at all. Some have forgotten how to smile, and it actually hurts them to smile, or to see others do so.

The thought of fear is everywhere...The more sensitive you are to the impress of thought, the more liable are you to be affected by this thought current of fear until your spirit, by constant demand of the Supreme Power, builds up for itself an armour of thoughts positive to this current and one that will deny it access.

A fanatic predicts a great catastrophe. The sensational newspapers take up the topic, ventilate it, and affect to ridicule but still write about it. This sets more minds to thinking and more people to talking. The more talk the more of this injurious force is generated. As a result thousands of people are affected by it unpleasantly, some in one way, some in another, because the whole force of that volume of fear is let loose upon them.

The more impressionable you are to the thought about you, the more are you liable to be thus affected... you can train your mind to shut out this thought.... And it keeps it open only to strength. You can do this by cultivating the mood of drawing to yourself and keeping in the mood and current of thought coming of God or the Supreme Power for good.

The more you get into the thought current coming from the Infinite Mind, making yourself more and more a part of that mind...the quicker you are freshened, and renewed physically and mentally. You become continually a newer being. Changes for the better come quicker and quicker.

Your power increases to bring results. You lose gradually all fear as it is proven more and more to you that when you are in the thought current of Infinite good there is nothing to fear. You realize more and more clearly that there is a great power and force which cares for you. You are wonderstruck at the fact that when your mind is set in the right direction all material things come to you with very little physical external effort.

You will see in this demand for the highest good that you are growing to power greater than you ever dreamed of. It will dawn on you that the real life destined for the awakened few now, and the many in the future is a dazzling dream-a permanent realization that it is a happiness to exist--a serenity and contentment without abatement--a transition from pleasure to pleasure, and from the great to greater pleasure.

You find as you get more and more into the current of the Infinite Mind that exhausting toil is not required of you, but that when you commit yourself in trust to this current and let it bear you where it will, all things needful will come to you.

There is no limit to the power of the thought current you can attract to you nor limit to the things that can be done through the individual by it. In the future some people will draw so much of the higher quality of thought to them, that by it they will accomplish what some would call miracles. In this capacity of the human mind for drawing a thought current ever increasing in fineness of quality and power lies the secret of what has been called "magic."

Chapter Four - ONE WAY TO CULTIVATE COURAGE.

COURAGE and presence of mind mean the same thing. Presence of mind implies command of mind...

You can cultivate courage and increase it at every minute and hour of the day. You can have the satisfaction of knowing that in everything you do you have accomplished two things--namely, the doing of the thing itself and by the manner of its doing, adding eternally to yourself another atom of the quality of courage. You can do this by the cultivation of deliberation--deliberation of speech, of walk, of writing, of eating--deliberation in everything.

You will remember that anything which is done in mind, expends quite as much force as if done with the body.....

No man makes or invents a truth. Truth is as general and widely spread and belongs to every individual as much as the air we breathe...Above all demand more and more courage of the Supreme Power.

Tools to pick from this chapter is to deliberately choose your behaviours, "deliberation of thought" Also, just as many other authors have said "anything that is done in mind, expends as much force as if done with the body". Remember the athletic testing, the same muscles had impulses whether working physically or visualizing the event.

Chapter Five - LOOK FORWARD

THE tendency with many people after they are a little "advanced in years" is to look backward with regret. The "looking" should be the other way--forward.

It is one chief characteristic of the material mind to hold tenaciously to the past. It likes to recall the past and mourn over it. The material mind has a never-ending series of solemn amusement, in recalling past joys, and feeling sad because they are never to come again. But the real self, the spirit, cares relatively little for its past, it courts change. It expects to be a different individual in thought a year hence from that it is today.

It is willing a thousand years hence to forget who or what it is today, for it knows that this intense desire to remember itself for what it has been retards its advance toward greater power and greater pleasure. What care you for what you were a thousand or five thousand years ago?

Those selves, those existences, have done their work for you. In doing that work they brought you possibly more pain than pleasure. Do you want to ever bear with you the memory and burden of that pain? If you can fling it off, demand of the Supreme Power aid to help you do so, and such aid will come.

Your spirit demands for the body it uses grace, agility of movement and personal beauty, for it is made in the "image of God," and the infinite mind and life, beauty, grace and agility are the characteristics of that mind. In that phase of existence we called childhood and youth, the spirit has the chance to assert its desire for beauty and agility, because it has not as yet loaded up with false beliefs and regrets.

God never mourns or regrets. You as a spirit are made in His image. God is eternal life, joy and serenity. The more of these characteristics you reflect the nearer are you to the Infinite Spirit of Good.

Have you buried your dearest on earth? You do them no good by your sad thoughts concerning them. Your friend is not dead. It is only the body he used that lies there. We need as much as possible to fasten our thought on life and increasing life--life greater in its activity than any we have ever realized. That is not gained by looking backward. **Look forward.**

Every regret; every mournful thought; takes so much out of your life.

Nothing in Nature--nothing in the Universe is at a standstill. Nothing goes backward. A gigantic incomprehensible Force and Wisdom moves all things forward toward greater and higher powers and possibilities. You are included in and are a part of this Force. There is of you in embryo the power of preventing the physical body your spirit uses from decaying, and the power also of using it in ways which even the fiction of today would discard as too wild for the pages of the novel.

Regret is an inverted force--a turning of the mind to look backward when its natural and healthy state is to look forward, and live in the joys that are certain to come when we do look forward.

In the new life come to our race, when we have learned to be ever looking forward to the greater joys to come and cease to look backward and drag the dead past with us, men and women are to have bodies far more beautiful and graceful than those of today. Because their bodies will image or reflect their thoughts, and their thoughts will ever be fixed on what is beautiful and symmetrical. They will know that what is to come and what is in store for them out of the richness of the Infinite mind must exceed anything they have realized in the past.

You can have all the playfulness of youth with the wisdom of maturity. To have a clear powerful mind you need not be an owl.

Power comes of looking forward with hope--of expecting and demanding the better things to come. That is the law of the Infinite Mind, and when we follow it we live in that mind. Nature buries it's dead as quickly as possible and gets them out of sight. It is better, however, to say that Nature changes what it has no further use for into other terms of life.

The science of happiness lies in controlling our thought and getting thought from sources of healthy life.

Mulford's message here is to always look forward, power comes from looking forward. Health and Happiness is achieved in controlling our thoughts.

Chapter Six-GOD IN THE TREES; OR, THE INFINITE MIND OF NATURE.

Love is an element which though physically unseen is as real as air or water. It is an acting, living, moving force, and in that far greater world of life all around us, of which physical sense is unaware, it moves in waves and currents like those of the ocean.

The ways of God are unsearchable and past finding out. They are not for us to fathom. They are for us only to find out and live out, in so far as they make us happier. There is for all in time a serenity and "peace of mind which passeth understanding;" but this peace cannot be put through a chemical analysis or the operation of a dissecting room.

As the Great Spirit has made all things, is not that All Pervading Mind and wisdom in all things?

THE ANSWER: THOUGHTS ARE THINGS

Do we expect to find God, realize him more every day, appreciate the mighty and Immeasurable Mind more every day, and get more and more of His Power in us every day only by dwelling on the word of three letters, G-o-d.

The tree is then literally one of God's thoughts. That thought is worth our study. It contains some wisdom we have not yet got hold of. We want that wisdom. We want to make it part of ourselves. We want it, because real wisdom and truth brings us power. We want power to give us better bodies, sounder bodies, healthier bodies. We want entire freedom from sickness. We want lighter hearts and happier minds.

WE want a new life and a new pleasure in living for each day. We want our bodies to grow lighter, not heavier with advancing years. We want a religion which will give us certainty instead of hopes and theories. We want a Deity it is simply impossible to doubt. We want to feel the Infinite Mind in every atom of our beings. We want with each day to feel a new pleasure in living and, commencing where we left off yesterday, to find something new in what we might have thought to be "old" and worn out yesterday. When we come into the domain of the Infinite Mind and are ever drawing more of that mind to us and making it a part of us, nothing can seem "flat" stale and unprofitable"

We want powers now denied the mortal.

The nearer we are to a conception of the Infinite Mind--the clearer it is seen by us that this mind pervades all things--the closer we feel our relationship to the tree, bird or animal as a fellow creature, the more can we absorb of the vitalizing element given out by all these expressions of mind.

We get the element of love only in proportion as have it in us. We can only draw this element from the Supreme Power. We draw it in proportion as we admire every expression of the Infinite, be that expression tree, or shrub, or insect, or bird, or other form of the Natural.

Here Mulford speaks of the powers of God through the Creation of Nature and the importance of love. Loving Nature will bring you closer to loving the Infinite Mind that created Nature. It will bring you closer to achieving and sharing the Power from the Creator.

Chapter Seven - SOME LAWS OF HEALTH AND BEAUTY

YOUR thoughts shape your face, and give it its peculiar expression. Your thoughts determine the attitude, carriage, and shape of your whole body.

The law for beauty and the law for perfect health is the same. Both depend entirely on the state of your mind: or in other words, on the kind of thoughts you most put out and receive.

Your body is the actual clothing, as well as the instrument used by your mind or spirit. It is the same instinct, or higher reason making you like a well-formed and beautiful body, that makes you like a new and tasteful suit of clothes.

Does not refinement imply greater power, as the greater power of the crude iron comes out of the steel; and are not these greater and as yet almost unrecognized powers to come out of the highest and most complex form of known organization, man; and are all of man's powers yet known?

But it is the law of Nature, that every demand, silent or spoken, brings its supply of the thing wished for in proportion to the intensity of the wish, and the growing numbers of wishing; who, by the action of their minds upon some one subject, set in motion that silent force of thought, not as yet heeded in the world's schools of philosophy, which brings the needed supply.

There are two kinds of age--the age of your body, and the age of your mind. Your body in a sense is but a growth, a construction, of today, and for the use of today. Your mind is another growth or construction millions of years old. It has used many bodies in its growth.

You are not young relatively. Your present youth means that your body is young. The older your spirit, the better and better you preserve the youth, vigour, and elasticity of your body. Because the older your mind, the more power has it gathered from its many existences. You can use that power for the preservation of beauty, of health, of vigour, of all that can make you attractive to others.

That power is your thought. Every thought of yours is a thing as real, *though you cannot see it with the physical or outer eye, as a tree, a flower, a fruit. Your thoughts are continually molding your muscles into shapes and manner of movement in accordance with their character.*

If your thought is always determined and decided, you step in walking will be decided. If your thought is permanently decided, your whole carriage, bearing and address will show that if you say a thing you mean it.

If your thoughts are permanently cheerful, your face will look cheerful.

…your thought; and as you put it out or think it, by the inevitable Law of nature it attracts to it the same kin of thought-element from others.

You are then charging your magnet, your mind, with its electric thought-current…and the law and property of thought connects all the other thought-currents.

Of whatever possible thing we think, we are building, in unseen substance, a construction which will draw to us forces or elements to aid us or hurt us, according to the character of thought we think or put out.

Make for yourself a plan for being always healthy, active, and vigorous, and stick to that plan, and refuse to grow decrepit, and refuse to believe the legions of people who tell you that you must grow old, you will not grow old. If you in your mind are ever building an ideal of yourself as strong, healthy and vigorous, you are building to yourself of invisible element that which is ever drawing to you more of health, strength, and vigour.

You can make of your mind a magnet to attract health or weakness.

Persistency in thinking health, in imagining or idealizing yourself as healthy, vigorous, and symmetrical, is the cornerstone of health and beauty. Of that which you think most, that you will be, and that you will have the most of.

One key thing from this chapter is how we can help to manage this body, this shell that houses our brain, our conscious, our soul. It is a house that by persistent thought of health and wholeness, we can keep in better shape than it would be if we ignore it. Without our forward thought of "vigour", the body will fall into the status quo pattern of ageing as the years pass.

Again Mulford speaks of that Power of your Thought. Every thought of yours is a thing, is real even though you cannot see it. Charge your magnet, your mind to connect with other thought currents.

Chapter Nine- THE GOD IN YOURSELF

As a spirit, you are part of God or the Infinite Force or Spirit of good. As such part, you are an ever-growing power which can never lessen, and must always increase, even as it has in the past through many ages always increased, and build you up as to intelligence, to your present mental stature. The power of your mind has been growing to its present quality and clearness through many more physical lives than the one you are now living. Through each past life you have unconsciously added to its power.

For the aim of living is happiness. The God in yourself--the ever-growing power in yourself--has made you see incompleteness in your character; yet that incompleteness was never so near a relative completion as now.

Of this the greatest proof is that you can now see what in yourself you never saw or felt before.

...you are one of the "temples of God" ever being built by yourself into ever-increasing splendor.

THE ANSWER: THOUGHTS ARE THINGS

What is the aim of life? To get the most happiness out of it, to so learn to live that every coming day will be looked for in the assurance that it will be as full, and even fuller, of pleasure than the day we now live in; to banish even the recollection that time can hang heavily on our hands;

To be thankful that we live; to rise superior to sickness or pain, to command the body, through the power of the spirit so that it can feel no pain, to control and command the thought so that it shall ever increase in power to work and act separate, apart, and afar from our body, so that it shall bring us all that we need of house or land or food or clothes, and that without robbing or doing injustice to anyone;

To gain in power so that the spirit shall ever recuperate, reinvigorate, and rejuvenate the body so long as we desire to use it, so that no part or organ shall weaken, wither, or decay;

To be learning ever new sources of amusement for ourselves and others; to make ourselves so full of happiness and use for others, that our presence may ever be more welcome to them; to be no one's enemy and every ones' friend,-- that is the destiny of life in those domains of existence where people as real as we, and much more alive than we, have learned, and are ever learning, how to get the most of heaven out of life. That is the inevitable destiny of every individual spirit.

You cannot escape ultimate happiness and permanent happiness as you grow on and on in this and other existences.

And the more sensitive you grow, the more clearly will you see the law which leads away from all pain, and ever toward more happiness, and to a state of mind where it is such an ecstasy to live, that all sense of time is lost--as the sense of time is lost with use when we are deeply interested or amused, or gaze upon a thrilling play or spectacle--so that in the words of biblical record, "a day shall be as a thousand years, and a thousand years as a day."

The Nirvana of the Hindus suggests that all the possibilities of life coming to our planet--"Nirvana" implying that calmness, serenity, and confidence of minds which comes of the absolute certainty that every effort we make, every enterprise we undertake, must be successful...

Before men knew how to use electricity there was as much of it as today, and with the same power as today; but so far as our convenience was concerned it was quite useless as a message-bearer, lack of knowledge to direct it. **The tremendous power of human thought is with us all today very much in a similar condition. It is wasted, because we do not know how to concentrate and direct it.**

To say anything is impossible because it seems impossible to you, is just so much training in the dangerous habit of calling out "Impossible" to every new idea. "All things" are possible with God. God works in and through you. To say "Impossible!" is to what you may do or become is a sin. It is denying God's power to work through you. It is denying the power of the Infinite Spirit to do through you far more than what you are now capable of conceiving in mind.

When you say "Impossible!" and "I can't" you make a present impossibility for yourself. This thought of yours is the greatest hindrance to the possible.

Christ's spirit or thought had power to command the elements, and quiet the storm. Your spirit as part of the great whole has in the germ, and waiting for fruition, the same power. Christ, through power of concentrating the unseen element of his thought, could turn that unseen element into the seen, and materialize food--loaves and fishes.

That is a power inherent in every spirit, and every spirit is growing to such power. You see today a healthy baby-boy. It cannot lift a pound; but you know there lies in that feeble child the powers and possibilities which, twenty year hence may enable it to lift with ease two hundred pounds. So the greater power, the coming spiritual power, can be foretold for us, who are now relatively babes spiritually.

The law cannot be entirely learned by us out of past record or the past experience of anyone, no matter to what power they might have attained.

THE ANSWER: THOUGHTS ARE THINGS

You must study and find out for yourself what your nature requires to bring it permanent happiness. You are a book for yourself. You must open this book page after page and chapter after chapter, as they come to you with the experience of each day, each month, and each year and read them. No one else can read them for you as you can for yourself.

No one else can think exactly as you think, or feel just as you feel, or be affected just as you are affected by other forces or persons about you; and for this reason no other person can judge what you really need to make your life more complete, more perfect and more happy so well as yourself.

The Christ of Nazareth once bade certain of his followers not to worship him. "Call me not good" said he. "There is none good save God alone." Christ said, "I am the way and life," meaning, as the text interprets itself to me, that as to certain general laws of which he was aware, and by which he also as a spirit was governed, he knew and could give certain information. But he never did assert that his individual life, with all the human infirmity or defect that he had "taken upon him," was to be strictly copied.

He did pray to the Infinite Spirit of Good for more strength, and deliverance from the SIN of FEAR when his spirit quailed at the prospect of his crucifixion; and in so doing, he conceded that he, as a spirit (powerful as he was) needed help as much as any other spirit; and knowing this, he refused to pose himself before his followers as God, or the Infinite, but told them that when they desired to bow before that almighty and never to be comprehended power, out of which comes every good at the prayer or demand of human mind, to worship God alone,--God, the eternal and unfathomable moving power of boundless universe; the power that no man has ever seen or ever will see.

That Power is today working on, and in, and through, every man, woman, and child on this planet. Or, to use the biblical expression, it is, **"God working in us and through us." We are all parts of the Infinite Power--** *a power ever carrying us up to higher, finer, happier grades of being.*

Chapter Ten - THE HEALING AND RENEWING FORCE OF SPRING

If you will but entertain this idea of spring's renewing force respectfully, though you cannot believe it thoroughly at first, you will receive much help by such respectful entertainment; for if you do not kick a live truth out of your mind when it first presents itself, it will take root and live there and prove itself by doing you good.

In the kingdom of nature, we find periods of rest constantly alternating with periods of activity.

When man recognizes the fact that he cannot use his body year after year.... and when he does recognize the fact that through placing himself oftener in restful and receptive states, as do tree, bird, and animal in their natural state, he will then, through receiving far more of this element, enjoy a far greater health of body, elasticity of muscle, vigour and brilliancy of mind. He would also have other senses and powers awakened within him, whose existence is still doubted by most people.

The thought-power which works most while the body is relatively inactive is really the strongest and ultimately prevails. It is subtle, noiseless, unseen.

> "What power is this?" you ask--"How gained? How developed?" It is the power of minds united on one purpose, in perfect concord, and who do not use it all in physical activity.

..Get into that state of repose when your thought-power could work at a distance and apart from you body, and bring you in time a hundred-fold more of beneficial result than can ever be realized through mere physical exertion.

If you are in conditions of life where at present it is impossible to give yourself needed rest and you feel thoroughly the need of such rest, you may rely upon it that your persistent desire, your prayer, your imperious demand that you shall have opportunity to so profit by them. When any need is thoroughly felt, the thought and desire coming of such a feeling is itself a prayer--a force which will bring you help and take you out of injurious surroundings and modes of *life. We repeat this assertion often. It needs frequent repetition. It is the mainspring of all growth and great law in the words.*

> *"Ask, and ye shall receive: seek, and ye shall find, knock and it shall be opened unto you." He wisely made no attempt to explain this mystery whereby earnest human thought, desire, or aspiration always in time brings the thing or result desired.*

We say, "Wind is air in motion" What sets it in motion, and keeps it in motion? ...What power keeps our lungs breathing day and night, or the blood running to every part of the body? Are not all of these of the power of God, or the infinite spirit or force of good, working within you as it works in everything that lives and grows? Only to us is at least given the knowledge to work this power intelligently.

Chapter Eleven - IMMORTALITY IN THE FLESH

This possibility must come in accordance with the law that every demand or prayer of humanity must bring supply.

Faith means power to believe in the true, or the capacity for the mind to receive true thoughts. The faith of Columbus in the existence of a new continent was a power in him to entertain such idea greater than others of his time. People who use the common expression "has faith in themselves," have also an actual power for carrying out their undertakings greater than those who have no faith in themselves.

When you demand faith in possibilities for yourself that now seem new and strange; you demand also, the power and ability to draw to you the capacity to see and feel reasons for truths new to you. If you demand persistently the truth and only the truth you will get it, and the whole truth means power to accomplish seeming impossibilities.

ASK, BELIEVE, & RECEIVE

"Thy faith hath made thee whole" said the Christ of Judea to a man who was healed. To us this passage interprets itself as meaning that the person healed had an innate power of believing that he could be healed. This power was of his own spirit (and not of Christ's) so acted on his body instantly to cure his infirmities. Christ was a means of awakening this power in that man's spirit. But Christ himself did not give the person that power. It was latent in the person healed. Christ woke it into life.

No person can become permanently whole (which implies among other powers, immortality in the flesh) and have entire and permanent freedom from disease, who is ever trusting, or leaning on any other save the Supreme to gain the power of faith. In this respect every mind must stand entirely alone. You cannot draw the highest power if you depend always for help from another or others. If you do you are only borrowing or absorbing their faith. Such borrowed faith may work wonders for a time, but it does not come to stay.

Our most profitable demand or prayer made consciously or unconsciously is "Let my faith be ever increased."

…the eternal fact that all things in this planet are ever moving forward to greater refinement; greater powers; and greater possibilities.

A body thus ever renewing, beautifying, freshening and strengthening means a mind behind it ever renewing with new ideas, plans, hope, purpose and aspiration. Life eternal is not the half dead life of extreme old age.

When the Christ of Judea said to the elders of Israel of the little child, "Except ye become as this child ye cannot enter the Kingdom of Heaven," he meant as the text interprets itself to us, that they should become as open to that inflowing of force as that spirit (the child) was at that period of its existence. Were such influx maintained, the youth of the body would be perpetual.

Chapter Twelve - THE ATTRACTION OF ASPIRATION

...when spirit gains the ascendancy... We see then clearly the good in all. We are thereby attracted more or less to all. And as we find the good in all, we get good, from all. We love more than we hate.

To be able to admire, to have the clear sight to detect he good in the lowest nature and to keep the evil out of sight, is a source to us of strength, of health, of continual increase of power. Love is power. You are always the stronger when in a condition of admiration.

Attraction is the Law of Heaven. Spirituality is attracted to what it finds of itself anywhere. It sees the diamond in the rough, though embedded in the coarsest mold.

Divinity is also contagious. Goodness is catching. In good time the world will learn that health is also.

There cannot be the highest health and vigour without aspiration and purity of thought. Pure thought brings the purest blood.

With an ever increasing purity of thought, cleanliness and care for the body will come as a natural result. The vessel will clean itself. Diet will be regulated by the natural demand of appetite.

It is this aspiration for the highest and best that in time causes an actual new birth of the body--a total "reformation" throughout in the quality and composition of flesh, bone, blood, muscle and sinews, a change in the material organization corresponding with that of the spiritual.

The path of self-healing lies in the calling for the elements of health and strength, to drive out disease. That is you pray for such elements and they come to you. Strength or vigour is an element of spirit or more refined matter. The more often is our will exercised in praying for it the quicker will it come.

Keep it (your mind) as much as you can on the thought of strength, vigour, health, activity. *As aids to erect this frame of mind, fix it as much as you can on illustrations and symbols of Nature's force and power, on storm and tempest, on the heaving billow and majesty of the Ocean, on the Morning Sun rising in all his glory to refresh and invigorate man, animal and vegetation*

If there be in prose or poetry any illustrations of this character which affect you strongly, recur to them. Read them aloud or in silence. Because in doing so you are setting the mind in the right direction to receive strength. In brief think of strength and power and you will draw it to you. Think of health and you get it.

A relatively perfected life means a life ***whereby a mind or spirit has grown to, or gathered so much power by simply asking or praying for power; or in other words, setting that mind as a magnet in the proper attitude to attract power,*** *that it shall be able constantly to recuperate or make over the body with fresher, newer, and finer material, and also to put this body on or take it off, materialize it with pleasure, as did the Christ immediately after his crucifixion. The Jews had only destroyed his material body. The spirit of Christ had power to re-clothe itself with a new body. Of this another record illustration is the Prophet Elijah's translation to Heaven.*

The Attraction of Aspiration - Every thought or desire of ours to be nobler, more refined, freer, from malice, ill-will toward others, and to do others good without exacting conditions on a thing, a force of unseen element which does actually tend or draw upward...

This, the aspiring order of thought you draw from the higher realms of spirit or element every time you wish, pray or desire it. You are drawing to you then, that of unseen element which incorporates itself with your body and spirit, and it then commences literally to draw you toward the realm and element of greater, broader, pure life existent in zones or bands about our planet. It will, as you persist in this aspiring thought, make you stand more erect. The phrase "the upright man" or woman implies that the effect of this unseen element so brought you of aspiration makes you physically as well as spiritually upright.

As you are ruled more and more by the attraction of aspiration, the desire to be more and more of a God or Goddess, the determination to conquer all the evil within you, which is the only way to conquer any and all evil outside of you, your form will in accordance grow more upright, your eye will be more open and uplifted, your heart will be "lifted up," your cheeks will bloom with fresher colour, your blood will fill more and more with a finer and powerful element, giving to your limbs strength, vigour, suppleness and elasticity of movement. You are then filling more and more with the Elixir of Life, which is no myth by a spiritual reality and possibility.

The ending of the body of the future will be the birth or development of a new physical body for which the old one shall serve as a shell or envelope until the new one is ripe and ready to come forth in a manner analogous to the development of the moth or butterfly from the cocoon.

Such growths and transitions will take place at lesser and lesser intervals, until at last the spirit will grow to such power that it can will and attract to itself instantly out of surrounding elements a body to use so long as it pleases on this stratum of life.

This is the condition foreseen by Paul when he said "O Death, where is thy sting? O grave, where is thy victory? And again where he writes, "The last great enemy which shall be overcome is Death."

We quote Paul, because no ancient teacher has more plainly foreshadowed these possibilities than he. Undoubtedly they were known to others both of the recorded and unrecorded human history of this planet which stretches back to periods far more remote than those inferred in the Mosaic creation.

These truths, these possibilities for avoiding decay, death and pain, and growing into and taking on a newer and newer body, and newer, fresher and more vigorous life, vitally affect us of today. We must not regard these statements as affecting only a coming race of people of some far distant future. They affect us.

They are possibilities for us. We have belonging to us the powers for bringing to us new life and new bodies. If you are not told of these your powers how can you ever use them?

You cannot accumulate your neighbour's powers; you can only grow and use yours alone.

We live surrounded by the same elements, and we are in possession of the same powers to greater or lesser extent, whereby three young Jews passed unharmed through a fiery furnace--whereby the Prophet Daniel, through exercise of the superior force of human thought, quelled the ferocity of the lions in the den; whereby Paul shook off the serpent's venom; whereby the Man of Nazareth perform his wonderful works.

"Was this not God's power?" you ask. Yes, the power of God or the Infinite and incomprehensible spirit of Eternal Good working in and through these His children, as the same power can work in and through us the more we call it to us, *over the lower or cruder mind.*

All seen element, or as we call it matter, is expression of the lower or cruder mind. Rocks, hills, clouds, waves, trees, animals and men, are all varying expressions of the lower cruder mind.

The power of mind over matter means the power of the higher mind over all these expressions of the lower mind.

The aspiration, the earnest prayer or demand to be better, to have more power, to become more refined, will bring more and more of the finer elements and forces; that is spirit to you. But the motive must be the natural heart-felt zealous wish to impart what you receive to others.

You cannot call the fullness of this power to you if you intend living only for self. You may get it to a degree and accomplish much by it. Your demand if living only for self may bring to you houses, wealth and fame. But the demand based on the selfish motive will in the end bring only pain, disease and disappointment.

Chapter Thirteen: THE ACCESSION OF NEW THOUGHT

NEW thought is new life.

So we do not live by bread alone. But our natures demand ever new and newer food of thought.

Call then, all new thought, and if you please new emotion, food--food as necessary to make the relatively perfect physical and mental man or woman as is the bread we eat. We desire ever fresh food; we similarly desire and need always new and fresh thought.

The consciousness of such never-ending growth of improvement is also food for the growing mind, other than bread. Yet it is bread. It is the

"Bread of Life," and to be desired as "Our Daily Bread."

Would not also the thought each morning that a Great Power, an infinitely wise mind, as always ready to give more knowledge to help you through troubles--troubles from without and troubles from within. Would not such thought, and the trust begotten of it, be as food, strength, and healthy stimulation?

Especially when the reality of this Power and its ability to aid had been proven to you many times, so that the hope had become a conviction?

Are we yet fully awakened to the thought that we are receptacles for thought and with thought knowledge, and with knowledge Power, and that our capacity for receiving all these may be limitless, and that the supply of knowledge, power, new thought in the Universe is limitless also, and that it is all ours to draw from, and that the Bank can no more break than Eternity can end.

All experiences are valuable for the wisdom they bring or suggest. But when you have once gained wisdom and knowledge from any experience, there is little profit in repeating it, especially if it has been unpleasant.

In all business we must press on in mind to the successful result. We must see in mind or imagination the thing we plan completed, the system or method organized and in working order, the movement or undertaking advancing and ever growing stronger and more profitable.

Forgetting the things behind and pressing on to those before is a maxim having a thousand intensely practical applications.

When you at the day's commencement in thought look before to a new thing, the thought of health and strength.....you are making the conditions for realizing such health and strength.

Life is a continual advance forward. If we are advancing forward, it is better to look forward. A mighty, eternal and incomprehensible force pushes us all forward.

Whatever the mind is set upon, or whatever it keeps most in view, that it is bringing to it, and the continual thought or imagining must at least take form and shape in the world of seen and tangible things. ...this fact is the cornerstone of your happiness or misery, permanent health and prosperity, or poverty. It needs to be kept as much as possible in mind.

Our thought is the unseen magnet, ever attracting its correspondence in things seen and tangible. As we realize this more and more clearly, we shall become more and more careful to keep our minds set in the right direction.
We shall be more and more careful to think happiness and success instead of misery and failure.

THE ANSWER: THOUGHTS ARE THINGS

When we realize that we can and do think ourselves into what we are, as regards health, wealth and position, we realize also that we have found in ourselves "the pearl of great price," and we hasten to tell our neighbor that he may seek and find in himself this pearl and power also….through the power it gives them to add to the general wealth and happiness.

Life is fuller of possibilities for pleasure than has ever been realized. The real life means a perpetual and ever increasing maturity.

Life means the development in us of powers and pleasures which in fiction in its highest flights has never touched.

It means an ever-increasing freshness, an ever-increasing perception and realization of all that is grand, wonderful and beautiful in the universe, a constantly increasing discovery of more and more that is grand, beautiful and wonderful, and a constantly increasing capacity for the emotional part of our natures to sense such happiness.

Life is eternal in the discovery and realization of these joys. Their source is inexhaustible. Their quality and character must be unknown until they reach us.

In the words of the Apostolic record, "Eye hath not seen nor ear heard, neither have entered into the heart of man the things which God hath prepared for them that love Him."

Through following the Spiritual Law, that peace of mind "which passeth all understanding" is in the future to come to many. That it has not in the past been realized is no proof it will not be. Life, then, whether its forces are in activity or rest, will be perpetual Elysium.

In the New Testament (the last revelation) we find the Christian and Apostolic teaching full of the sentiment of live, and life everlasting. Death is not argued or implied as an absolute necessity, but as an "enemy" which is ultimately to be destroyed. The dawn of such advent may be now.

It is now, not because of any one man's writings or assertions, but because many minds are now open to the reception of the greater revelation, which for centuries has been knocking at humanity's door, but could not enter by reason of the obtuseness and dull ear of those whom it sought to arouse and benefit.

'Why here under our noses is the greatest of all motive powers!

Why, human thought is a real element, a real force, darting out like electricity from every man's or woman's mind, *injuring or relieving, killing or curing, building fortunes or tearing them down, working for good or ill, every moment, night or day, asleep or awake, carving, molding, and shaping people's faces and making them ugly or agreeable.*

If you can build yourself up into a living power--if you can, with others, prove that physical health and vigour can take the place of old age--that all disease can be banished from the body--that material riches and necessities can come of laws and methods not now generally practiced.

Our more thoughtful people admit that by the time they have learned something of life, it is time to die.

Mankind demands something better. That demand, that cry has been swelling and increasing in volume for many centuries. Demand must always be answered. This demand is now being answered, first to a few, next the many.

New light, new knowledge and new results in human life and all it involves, are coming to this earth.

THE ANSWER: THOUGHTS ARE THINGS

Pull out insert to carry with you to keep your positive energy level up.

ANGEL NUMBERS…

Derivatives, doubles and triples of:

Zero, 0; is to be interpreted that Divine guidance of God or other ascended masters is right at hand to reassure you, to talk to you.

One, 1; in this instance, keep focussed on your positive desires as your thoughts are instantly manifesting.

Two, 2; is a message of "keep the faith", steady as you go; things are working out as they should. Keep believing in positive outcomes.

Three, 3; feel that you have a strong connection with God or with your chosen protecting ascended master, whether that is Jesus, Buddha or more. Feel loved, feel guided.

Four, 4; you are to think of angels being with you, around you. Ask for their help, feel secure and supported by heavenly beings.

Five, 5; Change is coming, always positive, but ask for help to manage the change. Sort of out with the old, in with the new, keep your happy thought strong to keep the change positive.

Six, 6; is a nudge that your thoughts are heavy with stress and fear, the material mind is too full of worry. The materialistic mind is suppressing the spiritual mind. Ask for help to strengthen your spiritual mind and bring it back to the forefront.

Seven, 7; lucky seven, keep up the great work, you are on the illuminated path. You are supported, doors of opportunity are opening.

Eight, 8; is a favourable sign of abundance, prosperity, auspicious and financial support for you. Think of money flowing in your direction.

Nine, 9; this is a game changer, a notification to get to work on your divine life purpose. You've completed the prerequisites, time to get ready for action steps. Ask your spiritual mind for what you need to motivate or clarify what to do.

ABOUT THE AUTHOR
MARION COLLIN

Marion Collin was born in the family farmhouse close to a small rural town and was raised by her widowed mother along with five older siblings. Yes, as the youngest, she was raised by them all and grew up with a large and wonderful extended family that included spouses of older siblings and many, many cousins from every branch of the family tree.

Even as a child she was writing short stories for school class work. Events later in Marion's life led her to "seek the answer" as to why some prayers had so clearly been answered. Yet, why weren't all her prayers answered in the way they were asked?

Many people have translated the Bible, but one message may have been overlooked. Researching led her through lost ancient writings; through one hundred year old readings; and modern day inspirational books. All seemed to be seeking knowledge; all seemed to have a common thread of wisdom that she now shares with you in this book.

Your mind, mindfulness meditation and powerful thinking with asking are a key. Recent scientific and medical research into the fantastic networks and functions of the brain is proving this to be true.

Marion and her husband live and raised their family in southern Alberta, Canada.

CPSIA information can be obtained at www.ICGtesting.com
Printed in the USA
LVOW07s2059070915

453180LV00001B/16/P